Joe Black

The Magic Within

Joe's Path of Survival and Self-Discovery

Written by Joe Black

ISBN: 9798343588903

Disclaimer

The names of the people in this autobiography have been changed to protect their identities.

Prolog

Let me start by saying something straight; I'm no saint. And honestly, I doubt anyone besides my mother ever thought I was. My ex-wives; they definitely wouldn't call me that. So, if you're reading this expecting some kind of redemption story or moral lesson, let me stop you right there. This isn't about painting my life as some grand, tragic, or heroic tale. It's just my life, as I saw it.

What I'm sharing here is not meant to convince you that I'm a good person or a bad human. I'm certainly not here to preach about right and wrong. What I am doing is telling the truth, at least my version of it. I guess I'm writing this more for myself than anyone else, as some kind of therapy, a way to make sense of things. You could call it a way to process, to confront the messes I've made and the demons I still wrestle with.

We all have those demons, don't we? I'm not pretending my struggles are any worse than yours. We all go through battles. I still fight mine every day, and who knows; maybe one day I'll win. Maybe that's what life is, a series of challenges, never-ending, until the story is done. You get through one, and another pops up, waiting for you. Life never really lets you rest long, at least, not until it doesn't anymore.

If you stick with me through these pages, maybe you'll recognize some of your own trials in my story. Maybe you'll even learn something to help you from my mistakes. What I hope most is that you get something out of it, even if it's just the understanding that none of us really know what the hell we're doing most of the time. We're all just trying to figure it out, stumble through, and make sense of the chaos.

I'm going to be brutally honest here, but I want to acknowledge something about honesty upfront; truth is a slippery thing. It's shaped by perspective, by how we see the world and how the world sees us. I've known plenty of people who struggle with the truth, and I think I understand why. Sometimes, it's hard to even know what the truth is. Life is messy, contradictory, and colored by the angle you're looking from.

Let me give you an example. Recently, I saw two photos of the same moment. The Prince of Wales, standing in front of a crowd. In one shot, taken from the side, it looked like he was flipping the crowd off, middle finger raised, and everything. The expression on his face didn't quite match the gesture, which made it all the more confusing. Then, right next to it, there was another photo, taken head-on. This time, it was clear he wasn't flipping off the crowd at all, he was showing off his new wedding ring. Same moment, two completely different perspectives and interpretations.

I've learned that life is a lot like that. The same event can seem completely different depending on where you're standing when it happens. From one angle, someone's a hero. From another, they're a villain. And maybe, when you read this book, you'll find yourself seeing me through one of those two lenses. Maybe you'll think I'm just another jerk, or maybe you'll see something redeemable. Either way, that's on you. I'm just here to tell you what happened, from where I stood.

Trying to sum up a lifetime in a single book isn't easy. There's no way I can capture every moment, but I'll try to cover the ones that mattered the most. Some of those moments I'm proud of, others… not so much. I've made my share of bad choices, ones that have cost me dearly. But I want to make one thing clear, I'm not here to make excuses or beg for forgiveness. I'm not a good man, not a bad man; just a man. Nothing more. A regular guy who's tried his best, screwed up along the way, and is still trying to figure it out.

So, if you're looking for a neat story about redemption or some grand moral arc, you might want to pick up another book. But if you're curious about what it's like to be just a man, living an imperfect life, struggling through the mess like everyone else, then keep reading. This is my story. No more, no less.

The Magic Within

Chapter 1

I suppose most people think about writing their life story before they die. For me, it seems I missed that deadline. Not just because I'm late in starting this, but because, well, I've already passed away. Yes, you read that right; I died. I don't think too many people can boast about telling their story after they've left this world.

Now, for most, death is the closing chapter, the full stop at the end of the book. But I've always heard that endings are just new beginnings, and I really hope that's true. Either we go on after this life in some new form, or we don't. I guess we'll all find out eventually, but I'm jumping ahead of myself. Every story needs a proper beginning, and I think you'll want to hear how I got to the point where my life ended.

To start with, I was born two weeks early; not quite a premature birth but early enough that I was very small. I was the first child of a middle-class family in Seattle, Washington. The oldest kid is often the experimental child for parents, an unintentional guinea pig as they figure out what being a mom and dad actually means. Is this just a grandiose theory? Well, I may have proved it to be true from the moment I entered this world. I shocked my parents right out of the gate.

Most parents pray for a healthy baby, and for mine, that prayer turned into immediate concern. Moments after I was born, the doctor noticed something was wrong. My right arm bore a bright red, raised ring of bunched skin, encircling the middle of my forearm. It was alarming, but after a careful examination, the doctor determined that despite the odd deformity, my arm worked just fine. No emergency surgeries or treatments were needed, and I would heal in time.

The doctor had a theory about what caused the ring of discolored tissue. He believed my arm had been broken in the womb, long before I ever took my first breath. My mother wasn't exactly surprised by this idea. She actually thought she had a pretty good idea of when it had probably happened as well. That spring, she had been walking two dogs for my grandmother, one large, one small. She was about six months pregnant with me at the time. It was a sunny, peaceful day, and everything was going fine until the small dog, hyper as ever, started running circles around her legs, wrapping her up in the leash. Just as she tried to untangle herself, the large dog took off after something, dragging her forward. With her legs tied together, she fell, hard, onto her stomach.

The pain was sharp, but after a short self examination she was sure she was alright. Her concern quickly turned to me, the child inside her. She couldn't be sure one way or the other if I had been injured or not. So she kept a careful eye on my movements in the days that followed. I still kicked now and then, so she assumed I was probably alright. When she saw my arm for the first time, though, she knew I'd been hurt. And while the injury wasn't life-threatening, it was a reminder that even before I was born, I had already survived my first brush with death. The reaper would make several visits to me over the years, this was just the first. It almost seemed like he was in a hurry to take me for some unforeseen reason that still alludes me to this day.

Some people might say I received a rough start in life, breaking my arm before I ever saw the light of day. But I prefer to think of it slightly differently; I survived. I could've died right then and there, and this story would have been over before it began. But I made it through my first meeting with the reaper, though it wouldn't be my last. To this day, I still carry the mark of that first dance with death; a large strawberry birthmark still circles my right arm, a faint echo of that early trauma. Fortunately, I never had any trouble with the arm itself. If the birthmark weren't there, I probably wouldn't even know that anything had ever happened. I'd say I was lucky. For now, anyway.

Chapter 2

When I was a young, my parents told me I was named after my dad. This confused me, because none of his legal names were Joseph, which is what they called me. The mystery didn't last long, though. My father, a devout Catholic, had taken the name Joseph at his baptism. Apparently, it was common for Catholics to pick a new name when they were baptized, as a symbol of starting a new life in Christ. My dad had chosen Joseph, after the biblical Saint Joseph.

And that's how I ended up being named after the earthly father of Jesus. Being named after a saint, however, doesn't mean you live like one. If you stick with this story, you'll quickly see I fell pretty far from that title. But even so, I always liked that connection, however distant it might seem from the life I actually lived. Because maybe, just maybe, even if you stumble through life like I did, there's something meaningful in the fact that you tried. Even if the story doesn't end the way you'd hoped.

* * *

The closest I ever came to sainthood was playing the part of one. Years later, I performed as Saint Joseph in a church play. For that brief time, I was Saint Joseph. But beyond that, I wouldn't say I lived up to the name. I wasn't a bad apple, but I was certainly no choir boy either. I also wouldn't say I was a troublemaker, quite the opposite in fact. I typically try to avoid trouble, but as you'll come to find out, trouble seems to have a way of finding me.

Around the time I was born, my parents bought a house on Delridge Way in Seattle, Washington. My dad worked tirelessly as an electrical apprentice, keeping the bills paid while my mom managed our growing family. And grow it did; quickly. A year and a half after I was born, my brother Ted came into the world. He was born a couple weeks late, the opposite of myself, so he was large. A year later, along came Sean. And then, only a year after Sean, my sister Kristen was born. She didn't even wait to get to the hospital, she was delivered in the back of a car. To say my parents were busy is an understatement.

One of my earliest memories is from the day Kristen was born. I can still remember my Aunt Janice in our kitchen, her face glowing with joy as she answered the phone to hear the news. It was a surreal moment, watching her expression light up as she found out about my sister's arrival. Kristen would be the last child born to my parents, and I for one, was glad to see the end of it.

Growing up on the rough streets of Seattle, our world felt small and confined compared to what my life would later become. Our house sat on a modest quarter-acre, with two levels and a small backyard where Ted and I often played. One day, while exploring the yard, we overturned an old tire that had been left to rot in the corner. As the tire rolled over, a whole ecosystem of bugs was revealed, crawling around in the damp hollow left behind.

Many of these insects were new to me, and I remember feeling both disgusted and fascinated as I studied them. But then, something happened that changed me forever.

Ted, always the bolder of the two of us, picked up one of the bugs; a long, brown creature with pincers at its rear, and said, "It's an earwig."

I'd never seen an earwig before, but the sight of the thing made my skin crawl. Without hesitation, Ted held it out toward me, tauntingly close.

"They crawl into your ear at night," he said with a wicked grin, "and lay eggs in your brain. When the eggs hatch, the babies eat your brain from the inside out."

I jumped back in horror, my heart racing as he teased me with the creepy creature. He continued to chase me around the yard, laughing as I darted away from the supposed brain-eater. I had no idea where he'd gotten that information. We didn't have the internet back then, not even computers. But whether it was true or not, it terrified me.

From that day on, earwigs became my personal nightmare; my mortal enemy. I couldn't get the image of them crawling into my ear and devouring my brain out of my head. Even now, the haunting thought still plagues me. I've spent much of my life with a deep, irrational fear of those tiny, creepy creatures. As I got older, I learned to manage it, but earwigs still make my heart race. And for years, I wondered if there was any truth to Ted's story.

Later, I found out the source of his gruesome tale; our mother. She'd told Ted that story, probably to get him to stay away from the bugs. Ted, of course, was only too happy to torture me with the this horror story. Brothers will be brothers, I guess. It wasn't until much later in life that I discovered the truth; earwigs don't typically crawl into people's ears, and they definitely don't lay eggs in anyone's brain. It was nothing more that an urban legend, one of those childhood myths that takes on a life of its own. When I finally read that, I can't tell you how relieved I was. I'd spent so many years fearing something that wasn't even real.

It's funny how fear works, isn't it? How your imagination can latch onto the most absurd things and hold us captive. Fear is one of the most powerful emotions we experience as humans, and it can be crippling. I suppose that's why fear is so often used to control people. Maybe one day, we'll be better at letting go of our irrational thoughts. In all honesty, I'm still working on it myself. But back then, all I knew was that earwigs were my sworn enemy, and the thought of them crawling into my head kept me up at night. Fear has a way of getting under your skin, sometimes literally.

Chapter 3

When I started kindergarten, I was a shy and nervous kid, unsure of how to navigate the new world of strangers around me. I'd always felt sheltered growing up, and social situations didn't come easily to me. The idea of meeting new people, learning to interact, and finding my place in this new environment made me anxious. I suppose that's not uncommon for kids, but this became a personal struggle that would follow me for most of my life.

Looking back, I used to blame my parents for this problem. It's a common enough theme among humans, blaming the people who raised us for the things we don't like about ourselves. I know now that it wasn't entirely their fault. They weren't social butterflies themselves, and without the skills to teach me, they could hardly be expected to prepare me for the wider world. I held onto that resentment for far too long, not realizing that they were doing the best they could with what they had.

Without good role models to guide me through the subtleties of social interaction, I was left to fend for myself, learning painfully slow and often feeling like I was out of place. I never quite got over that discomfort, even as I grew older. Parties and events always made me anxious, and that feeling of awkwardness became a constant companion throughout my life. It's one of the reasons I pursued the career that would define me later on, but I'm getting ahead of myself.

I discovered years later, during my time in college, that the number one fear among people is public speaking. Somehow, that comforted me, knowing that many others shared my struggle. I eventually stopped holding my parents accountable for my social shortcomings. After all, how could they teach something they themselves never learned? The burden of fixing my insecurities fell on me, and it took decades of painful lessons to get there.

The irony was that most things in life came easily to me. I excelled in science, math, and just about every subject; except one area. Spelling and reading were a constant challenge. I wasn't sure why, but no matter how much I tried, those skills always seemed out of reach. Unfortunately, my difficulty with reading fed into another issue; my obsessive-compulsive tendencies. I became fixated on my inability to read well, and it took me to a dark place. My self-esteem plummeted. I became convinced I was stupid, and from there, the downward spiral into depression began.

Physical challenges, on the other hand, were effortless. I could climb like a monkey, a fact that often worried my mother as I scaled fences, trees, and whatever else I could get my hands on. I was fast too, always darting through the neighborhood without a care. Walking to school was easy, the school was just a few short blocks away from our house, so the journey never felt like a chore.

But as the first day of kindergarten approached, I felt an overwhelming sense of anxiety. When I finally walked into that classroom filled with strangers, I was completely unsettled. Should I try to make friends? Should I keep to myself and wait for someone to approach me? I had no idea what to do. Despite my fears, in time, I managed to make a friend or two. I even started to enjoy myself during recess, playing with the few kids who had become my companions. But still, I couldn't shake the feeling that I was different. I wondered why some kids seemed so effortlessly popular, while I hovered somewhere in the middle, neither popular nor ostracized, just there. I suspect now that my self-centeredness didn't win me any points. It's a common affliction among young children I suppose, one I certainly wasn't immune to.

One of the early friendships I had was with a girl in my class. She seemed to take a particular interest in me, though at the time, I had little interest in girls. She would call my house frequently and engage me in conversation at school. Looking back, I think she liked me, but I was far too young to think much about that. I didn't mind talking to her, though our interests couldn't have been more different.

Boys and girls seem to think differently, even at that age. As we grew older, I lost contact with her when my family moved away. Sometimes, I catch myself wondering what might have happened if we had stayed in town. Would we have grown up together, maybe even become a couple in high school? Could we have gotten married one day? It's funny how the mind plays with "what ifs." Perhaps if I'd stayed, I wouldn't have had the relationship issues that plagued me as an adult. But those are questions with few answers.

What I do know is that I'll never find out what happened to her. I don't even remember her name, so looking her up in today's digital age isn't an option. All I have are the memories of a brief, innocent childhood friendship, one that faded with time but never entirely disappeared from my mind. That's the thing about childhood, though, it's full of fleeting moments that feel monumental at the time but are easily lost in the blur of growing up. Still, the few I do remember, like that friendship, are the ones that remind me how simple things once were. Before life got complicated, before fear and doubt set in, and before I became the man constantly working to fix the flaws I discovered too late.

Chapter 4

That year, one of the highlights was the annual school carnival. It was a dazzling event for a kid my age, full of games, rides, and strange attractions. I could hardly wait to explore it all. The atmosphere buzzed with excitement, and I felt like I was about to embark on the greatest adventure of my young life.

Each activity required tickets, so we waited in line to get a handful. While standing there with my folks, I watched the people ahead of us handing over their money and getting tickets in return. That's when something strange caught my attention. The first person in line gave the cashier a few dollar bills but only got back a couple of tickets and a few coins in change. Then, the next person handed over just one bill and got a huge stack of tickets, along with several bills in change. I stood there, utterly confused.

"Why was the second person treated better than the first?" I thought, my mind spinning with childish theories.

I was too young to understand that different bills had different values. To my untrained eyes, a dollar was just a dollar, and I had no concept of the variety of denominations. For a brief moment, I wondered if the cashier simply liked the second person better. It's funny to think back on how baffling that simple monetary exchange was to me then. I laugh at my younger self now, how could I have missed such an easy concept? But back then, I had bigger concerns, like which ride to go on first.

Once I put the confusing ticket situation behind me, my family and I had a fantastic evening. We played games, went on a few rides, and for a few hours, life felt easy and uncomplicated.

* * *

It's odd how certain memories stick with you, while others fade away. I can still remember the face of an old woman who lived a few houses down from us, although I'm terrible at remembering names. Hers, however, I never forgot; Mrs. Wilson.

There was something about her that made a lasting impression on me. She lived alone, in a rundown house that always seemed to be in a state of disrepair. My mother told me that Mrs. Wilson had once been married, but her husband had passed away, leaving her to fend for herself. Mrs. Wilson struggled to take care of her house, and even to care for herself. Out of kindness, my mom would bring her meals every day. Despite this, Mrs. Wilson never invited us inside. I always wondered why.

She had around twenty cats, maybe more, that roamed in and out of her house freely. They seemed to be everywhere, lounging on her porch, scattered across the lawn, hiding under bushes. Mrs. Wilson was the very definition of a "cat lady." I was always eager to go along with my mom when she dropped off the meals because I loved petting the kittens that swarmed her yard.

One day, while I was playing with one of the kittens, I picked it up to cuddle. It was small and soft, and for a moment, I was completely enchanted by how cute it was. But when it turned its head to look at me, I froze in horror. One of its eyes was missing; I panicked. The sight of that empty socket filled me with dread, and I dropped the kitten immediately, my heart racing. A creepy, irrational fear flooded my mind. Was it possible that whatever had happened to that kitten could happen to me too? Could I lose an eye just from touching it? My young mind raced with thoughts of unseen illnesses, and the idea of sharing that kitten's fate haunted me.

From that moment on, I hesitated to pet any of the kittens around Mrs. Wilson's house. My fear of something terrible happening to me took root, and even as the days passed, I couldn't shake the unsettling feeling.

Then came the day when everything changed. One evening, as usual, my mom and I walked over to Mrs. Wilson's house to drop off her meal. But this time, when we knocked, there was no answer. That was strange, Mrs. Wilson was always punctual about getting her food. My mom knocked again, louder this time, but still, nothing. Worry started to cloud my mother's thoughts. Something wasn't right.

After a few more knocks with no response, my mom decided to try the door; it was unlocked. She hesitated for a moment, then cautiously pushed it open. What she found inside was nothing like she had imagined. The house was in total disarray. Clutter and garbage were piled everywhere, stacked waist-high in some places. The smell was overwhelming, a thick stench that seemed to seep from every corner. Dust and cobwebs covered the walls, hanging down like eerie curtains.

I stayed near the doorway, too scared to go inside the spooky house. My mom moved deeper into the house, calling for Mrs. Wilson. It didn't take her long to find the old woman, lying face down on the floor. My mom rushed to her side and turned her over. To her horror, Mrs. Wilson let out a soft gasp, her chest moving slightly before she slumped back down. My mom jumped back, startled, but then realized what was happening. The gasping sound wasn't Mrs. Wilson breathing. It was just air escaping her lungs from the pressure of being moved. Mrs. Wilson was dead.

My mom quickly gathered herself and called 911, but there was nothing anyone could do. Mrs. Wilson was gone. It was the first time I had ever experienced death, and I didn't know how to process this new experience. What did it mean to be dead? I had no idea, but one thing I did know was that I didn't want it to happen to me. I wondered if death was contagious. Could just being near that house make me sick? Would I die too?

For days, I couldn't stop thinking about it. I remembered the one-eyed kitten and feared that maybe Mrs. Wilson had caught something from the cats. If she had, then I was doomed too. I had touched those kittens, after all. My young mind spiraled into irrational fears of illness and death. It took weeks for me to finally feel safe again, realizing that nothing had happened to me. I wasn't going to die from this.
Not yet, anyway.

Chapter 5

As a kid, I was full of energy, constantly moving, never content to sit still for too long. My parents, to their credit, did their best to channel that boundless energy into healthy outlets. One of their go-to spots for burning off my excess enthusiasm was the local Y.M.C.A. My dad, especially, would take us there to swim. We were usually required to wear life jackets, but as kids often do, I felt indestructible and impatient with rules meant to keep me safe. I wanted to prove something, prove I was big enough, strong enough to swim without any help.

One afternoon, I announced that I didn't want to wear my life jacket. My parents hesitated for a moment but eventually agreed. I must have been old enough by then, they figured. Or at least old enough to learn. As soon as we were at the pool, my younger brother Ted beelined for his favorite part; the water slide. It was the highlight of our trips to the "Y", and I was just as eager to join him. Ted went first, gleefully shooting down the slide and splashing into the pool below. My dad stood in the water a couple of feet from the base of the slide, ready to catch him. When Ted hit the water, he kicked his way toward our dad with impressive speed and confidence. I remember watching the look on my dad's face; surprised and proud that Ted has swam the short distance.

It was one of the few times I ever saw that kind of expression from him. My dad wasn't the kind of man who showed emotions easily, or at all, really. But in that moment, he couldn't help but let some of it slip through, praising Ted for how well he swam.

Suddenly, all I wanted in the world was to impress him too. I had to do more, be better. After all, I was the older brother. Ted's success only pushed me harder.

"Dad, move back a little!" I called out from the top of the slide, filled with a mix of excitement and determination.

I was going to swim farther than Ted, maybe even impress my dad more. I wanted to see that look of pride on his face directed at me. I went down the slide fast, the water rushing up around me as I splashed into the pool. The moment I hit the water, I began kicking, waving my arms furiously, determined to swim without help. I was desperate to show my dad what I could do; that I was the best. But then something went horribly wrong. Almost immediately, I realized I wasn't rising to the surface the way I thought I would. Instead of feeling the cool air on my face, I was sinking, the water pressing down on me from all sides.

I kicked harder, thrashed more wildly, my arms flailing in every direction. The surface seemed impossibly far above me, and no matter how hard I struggled, I wasn't getting any closer. Panic set in as I felt my lungs begin to burn. I was out of breath, and I hadn't even realized how fast it had happened. My muscles screamed, the fire in my chest spreading, my body betraying me with exhaustion and fear. I tried to fight it, but I was sinking deeper, losing control.

In that terrifying moment, a dark thought crept into my mind, I wasn't going to make it. I was about to drown. A sharp, suffocating fear of death gripped me, an abstract fear I hadn't fully yet understood. The more I fought, the weaker I felt, and the closer I seemed to drift toward that terrifying void I'd always heard about but never really thought could happen to me. I saw a tunnel closing in, darkness pulling me further under, and I wondered if I was about to find out what was on the other side of that tunnel.

Was this it? Was this where my short life would end? I had no idea what was coming, only that I was too young to go, but I was powerless to stop it from happening. Suddenly, a powerful hand grabbed my arm. The force of it startled me, jolting me from my daze. I was yanked upward, the water breaking around me as I was pulled to safety. I gasped in deep, desperate breaths of air, coughing, my chest aching but filled with sweet oxygen. My dad had gotten to me just in time.

"What took you so long?!" I yelled, my voice cracking with fear and embarrassment.

My dad chuckled softly, though I could tell he was still shaken by what had just happened. "You told me you wanted to swim," he said, almost as if it were no big deal. "It's okay. I got you."

He had saved me, but in my panic and shame, I couldn't appreciate it fully. Instead, I felt angry, at myself, at him, at the whole situation. I had wanted to impress him, but all I had done was make a fool of myself. In that moment, I was more scared of having failed in front of my dad than I was of drowning.

Looking back, I know I shouldn't have been mad at him. He'd saved my life, and I was lucky to be standing there, breathing in the fresh air. But I was young, scared, and embarrassed. I had bitten off more than I could chew, and my stubborn pride had almost cost me dearly. I wasn't the strong, capable swimmer I had imagined myself to be. Not yet, anyway.

That day, death knocked on my door but hadn't caught me. I'd escaped his clutches once again, thanks to my dad. But it was the first time I'd truly understood that death was out there, waiting for me. I had been lucky that day, but luck wouldn't save me forever. One day, death would catch up with me, as it does for everyone.

But not today.

Chapter 6

The following year, I entered first grade. It was an exciting time for me, not because of the schoolwork, but because of the activities and games we played. I loved running around during recess, and the social aspect of school was always more appealing than sitting still and studying. I wasn't much for focusing on lessons, easily distracted by anything more interesting than letters and numbers; which was almost everything. Despite my lack of effort, I picked things up quickly, at least in most subjects. But of course spelling and reading were a different story entirely.

No matter how hard I tried, I still struggled with reading and spelling. The words on the page seemed to shift and turn, the letters never staying still. They felt like they were playing tricks on me, flipping around and making it impossible for me to figure out which direction they were supposed to face. The letters "L," "E," and "R" gave me the most trouble, though sometimes, it felt like the whole alphabet was against me.

Even my teachers were confused by my difficulties. Back then, no one really seemed to know what dyslexia was or how it affected learning. They didn't appear to understand why a kid who could grasp math problems and other subjects with ease just couldn't get a handle on reading. It would be years before I finally understood what was going on, and why the simple act of reading felt like scaling a mountain.

Looking back, I'm surprised it took so long for anyone to figure it out. But in the meantime, my frustration grew. I started to hate reading, loathing every time I had to sit down and look at a page filled with words that seemed to mock me. Writing was no better, letters never stayed where they were supposed to, and I never knew if they were facing the right direction. I avoided both as much as possible. In fact, I hated reading so much that I didn't even bother with it during tests. It seemed easier to just guess the answers instead of trying to read the questions.

Guessing became my new strategy. I figured that with multiple choice tests, I had a one-in-four chance of getting the right answer. And surprisingly, I was a pretty good guesser. I almost always passed my tests, even if it was just by the skin of my teeth. On one occasion, I even managed to pull off a perfect score, and on one of the hardest tests of the year. Everyone, including the teacher, thought I had cheated. If only they had known the truth; I was just lucky.

It's funny how easily we can convince ourselves of things that aren't true. Because of my struggles with reading, I was sure I was stupid. I couldn't understand how everyone else in my class could read and write with such ease, while I struggled with something as simple as the alphabet. I figured I must be the problem. Believing I was dumb, I stopped trying altogether. Why bother when it was clear I couldn't succeed? That thought wormed its way into my mind and took root, slowly eroding my self-esteem. I spiraled into a dark place, filled with self-doubt and frustration.

But despite my difficulties in school, I had one thing going for me; I was a fast runner. I loved running, and in that, I excelled. I quickly became known as one of the fastest kids in my class. Every day, I raced down the sidewalks on my way home from school, sprinting the few blocks between school and home as if the wind itself couldn't catch me.

One day, after class, I took off for home at full speed, darting past other kids on the sidewalk, my feet pounding the pavement. I felt invincible. But in an instant, that feeling was ripped away. Suddenly, I was hit by something that knocked me senseless. My head spun, pain shooting through my body as I landed in the middle of the street. Dazed, I couldn't make sense of what had happened. I had no idea how I had ended up there, lying on the hard asphalt with cars passing dangerously close by.

Everything hurt. My head throbbed, my arm ached, and I could barely move. As my mind started to clear, I heard a voice, a young girl, probably around twelve, asking if I was okay. I couldn't understand her at first, but she seemed concerned and was trying to help. I must have been five at the time, and she seemed so much older to me then.

The girl helped me to my feet and guided me back onto the sidewalk. That's when I noticed the parked car just a few feet away, dangerously close to the spot I last remember being, and a man getting out in a hurry.

"Are you okay?" the man asked, looking worried as he approached us. I could barely process what he was saying.

"I know this boy," the girl told him confidently. "I'll take him home."

The man, clearly relieved that I was in someone else's care, didn't argue. He probably feared getting in trouble for hitting a kid with his car. Lawsuits must have flashed through his mind as he let us go without much protest. The girl walked me home, and when my mom opened the door, she told her what had happened.

My mom's face went pale as she pulled me inside and began checking me over. Miraculously, my injuries were minor, some bruises, a sore arm, and a nasty bump on my head. Looking back, it was a miracle I hadn't been hit by a second car while I lay in the street. If I had been, I might not be here to tell this story.

As my mom cared for me, the pain in my head faded a little, though I couldn't help but think that knock on the head might explain some of the bad decisions I'd make in the future. I'm joking, of course. But I did end up with a pretty big bump that day. Now, years later, it's easy to laugh about the incident. What was most important was I survived, and in time, the bump healed. But on that day, I learned how fragile life could be, and how quickly everything can change in the blink of an eye.

Chapter 7

It was an ordinary day when Ted and I made an exciting discovery in our house; the laundry chute. It was an unassuming metal slide, hidden behind a small door in the hallway, and it dropped straight from the first floor into the basement, where clothes usually tumbled down into a basket. But we saw it as something much more exciting; a secret slide.

Curiosity got the best of us. We opened the chute door and without a second thought, I climbed inside. With a whoosh, I slid down and landed on a soft heap of laundry below. Ted quickly followed, and we both erupted into fits of laughter. It was like having our very own amusement park ride inside our house, and we couldn't wait to go again.

After a few slides, we were caught in the act by our youngest brother, Sean. He had been watching us with wide eyes, curiosity clearly getting the best of him. Sean was still very young, not quite old enough to understand our antics, but eager to be a part of anything we found fun.

"Hey, Sean!" we called to him. "Want to try the fun slide?"

Sean looked nervous, his little face scrunched with uncertainty. We coaxed him, telling him how much fun it was, how easy. Slowly, Sean climbed halfway into the chute, but fear took hold and he froze. Ted and I exchanged impatient glances. He was holding up the fun. So, without thinking, we gave him a little push.

Down Sean went, sliding through the chute and landing softly in the pile of laundry. For a brief moment, I expected him to laugh, to find it just as fun as we did. But instead, Sean looked up at us, his eyes filled with fear. He didn't see the excitement we had promised; he was scared and unhappy. We didn't push him again after that. Sean refused to go near the chute after that day, and in hindsight, I felt bad about it. We hadn't meant to be bullies, but in our eagerness, we hadn't thought about how he might feel. I regretted pushing him, especially knowing what was to come later in my life. Bullying, even unintentionally, was never okay.

Ted and I, undeterred, continued our chute adventures. It was too much fun to stop. We even discovered that if we pressed our hands against the walls, we could stop ourselves midway down, hovering for a moment inside the chute like we were suspended in midair. It became a game, one of those childhood memories that would stick with me forever. We didn't know then, but those innocent days of playing and sliding down the laundry chute were fleeting.

* * *

That winter, Ted and I were playing in our room. Outside, snow fell in heavy flakes, and the house felt cold. To keep us warm, our mom had turned on the space heater. Ted and I, always full of ideas, decided to build a fort out of the blankets in the room. We draped them over chairs and beds, trying to create the perfect hideaway. In the midst of our building, we accidentally set one of the blankets on the space heater unaware of the danger.

We were too young and naive to understand the problems were were causing. Before we knew it, the blanket burst into flames. What started as a small flicker quickly grew into a roaring fire, consuming the blanket and spreading fast. We screamed in terror as the fire spread across the room, the heat and smoke filling the air. Panicked, we both scrambled onto our bunk beds, thinking that higher ground would keep us safe from the flames. I climbed to the top bunk, desperate to get as far from the fire as I could. But in my fear, I hadn't realized the danger that awaited me up there. The smoke was thickest at the ceiling, and I didn't know it could kill me faster than the flames.

Ted and I continued screaming for help, our voices choked by the dark smoke filling the room. The air was suffocating, and the fire seemed to close in around us. Then, through the chaos, our mom burst into the door. Her eyes widened in horror at the sight of the flames spreading across the room, the walls blackened by the thick smoke. Without hesitating, she grabbed two blankets that hadn't caught fire and began beating back the flames with all of her might. Desperation fueled her as she fought to save us, her fear evident in the way she moved, knowing that time was running out.

"Get down from the top bunk, Joe!" she screamed at me, her voice thick with panic.

At the time, I didn't understand why she wanted me down, closer to the flames. It didn't make any sense to me. I didn't know that the smoke rising to the ceiling was far more deadly than the fire below. I didn't realize that every breath I took filled my lungs with poison that could kill me if I stayed up there any longer; but my mom knew. She knew that if she didn't get me down soon, I might not make it.

I began coughing violently, the smoke clawing at my throat, my lungs burning with every breath. My mom worked faster, fear gnawing at her as she realized how close she was to losing us both. Finally, after what felt like an eternity, she managed to smother the flames and get me down from the bunk.

Outside, in the fresh air, I gulped down deep breaths, the burn in my lungs slowly fading. My mom had saved us; again. If she hadn't acted as quickly as she did, I don't know if I'd be here to tell this story. Death had come knocking at my door once more, but again, it left empty-handed. At this point, both my parents had saved me from the clutches of death, not once, but twice. I guess you could say I owed them both my life.

Chapter 8

I had never experienced magic before, at least not the kind that seemed to defy reality. Looking back now, it's almost laughable how easily amazed I was, but at that young age, I was spellbound. My dad knew one magic trick, and the first time he showed it to me, I was convinced that I had witnessed something that was truly a minor miracle.

We were in the living room, sunlight filtering through the curtains, casting a warm glow on the room. My dad stood there, holding a sock in his hand, his eyes twinkling with the kind of mischief I was too young to recognize. He rolled the sock up carefully, a slow and deliberate motion that already had me hooked. Then, with a sly grin, he placed the sock in his hand, closed his fingers around it, and slapped his palm a couple of times. And just like that, the sock was gone!

I sat there, wide-eyed and breathless, not quite believing what I had just seen. My dad, who had always seemed larger than life to me, had just performed real magic! I couldn't take my eyes off his hand, waiting for some clue, some explanation, but none came. I demanded he do it again, and again, and each time, the sock vanished without a trace. I had no idea how he was making it disappear. It was mesmerizing.

Most kids think their parents are the most incredible people in the world at that age, and I was no exception. My dad had just proven himself to be powerful, capable of wielding forces I couldn't understand. That one short performance sparked something inside of me; a fascination with illusion. I didn't know it yet, but that moment would mark the beginning of my lifelong obsession with magic.

A few years later, I watched a magician perform on The Muppet Show. His performance was nothing short of incredible, leaving me with the same sense of wonder I had felt that day in the living room with my dad. But this time, I felt something different; a yearning. I wanted to do what he did. I wanted to perform magic, to create awe and wonder in others.

I remember going up to my room after the show, my heart still racing, and kneeling beside my bed. I prayed, asking God to give me the ability to perform magic, just like the magician I'd seen on TV. I waited for an answer, hoping for a sign, but none came. Disappointed, I assumed my prayer had gone unheard, that maybe magic wasn't meant for me after all.

What I didn't know was that my prayer had been heard, in its own way. Years later, I would find myself performing tricks on stage, using my own hands to create illusions that would leave audiences wide-eyed, just as I had been when I watched my dad make that sock disappear. One day, I'd even perform a version of my dad's trick; only, I wouldn't use a sock.

* * *

Ted and I played together frequently, mostly because we had no-one else. Neither of us had many friends, but being so close in age and size made us perfect companions. Wherever I went, Ted followed. I didn't mind most of the time, he had no trouble keeping up with me, and we shared an unspoken bond that made our games feel like adventures.

One afternoon, boredom had set in, and I got the urge to do something daring. I jumped on the bed like any restless kid would, despite my father's warning not to do so. The mattress sprang under my weight, launching me back up into the air like a trampoline. The thrill of it made me laugh, and soon, Ted was at my side, joining in on the fun. We started competing, bouncing higher and higher, trying to outdo each other.

I was determined to prove I could jump the highest. Ted was getting some serious air, but I wasn't about to let him outshine me. That's when I noticed the headboard, a built-in bookshelf at the top of the bed. The idea hit me like a flash. If I jumped from there, I'd soar higher than Ted ever could. Without hesitation, I climbed onto the ledge and leaped off. My feet hit the bed, and I flew higher than ever.

Ted, not wanting to be outdone, decided to follow suit. He climbed up onto the headboard, ready for his big jump. But I couldn't let him win. The thought of Ted beating me was unbearable, so I did something impulsive, something I regretted the moment it happened.

Just as he was about to leap, I shouted, "Boo!"

Ted flinched in mid-air, his balance lost. Instead of landing squarely on the bed, he jumped at an odd angle and bounced off, crashing headfirst into the corner of the wall. The sound was sickening. His cry followed immediately, a sharp wail of pain that echoed in my ears.

I looked down at him, my heart sinking. Blood poured from a gash on his forehead, and I froze, unable to comprehend what had just happened. I'd never seen so much blood before. Panic surged through me, and I bolted down the stairs, shouting for help.

"Dad! Ted's hurt!" I cried, barely able to get the words out.

Ted stumbled behind me, tears streaming down his face, his little hand clutched to his bleeding head. My dad rushed over, pulling Ted's hand away to reveal the deep gash; his face darkened.

"What happened?" he roared.

"Joe did it!" Ted sobbed, pointing at me, his finger trembling.

Before I could explain, before I could say a word, my dad turned on me. He grabbed me by the front of my shirt, his grip tight and unyielding. For a split second, I thought he might be kidding, after all, I hadn't meant for Ted to get hurt. It was just an accident.

But my dad wasn't joking. In one swift motion, he lifted me up and threw me across the room. I hit the floor hard, the impact knocking the wind out of me. Stars danced in my vision, and for a moment, I lay there, stunned. I couldn't believe it. My own father had tossed me like I was nothing more than a sack of potatoes.

Even in my young mind, I knew I could have been seriously hurt, but the shock of the situation numbed everything. My dad's anger was palpable, but as soon as he tossed me aside, he turned his attention back to Ted, rushing him into the bathroom to clean his wound.

I stayed back, watching quietly from the hallway, guilt gnawing at me. I hadn't meant for any of this to happen. All I wanted was to win a silly jumping contest. Now, Ted had a gash on his head, and my dad's fury was still thick in the air.

To my surprise, Ted bounced back faster than I expected. Within minutes, he was running around the house again, the large bandage on his forehead the only sign of the accident. My parents had patched him up, and while I was relieved to see him playing like nothing had happened, I couldn't shake the weight in my chest.

Ted still blames me for the scar on his forehead, a constant reminder of that day. Part of me doesn't blame him, it was my fault, after all. I startled him, I pushed too far. But another part of me knows it was just an accident, a mistake born from childish competition.

That day, I learned a hard lesson. Sometimes, your actions, no matter how harmless they seem, can have dire consequences you never see coming.

Chapter 9

Ted and I were were often mischievous, but we tried our best to steer clear of real trouble. We knew what would happen if we didn't. My dad believed firmly in discipline, he was a devout Catholic who held tight to the saying, "Spare the rod, spoil the child." There was no way he was going to have spoiled kids in his house, and his punishments made sure of that. We did everything we could to avoid crossing him, but trouble has a way of finding us when we least expect it.

That summer, Ted and I were in the backyard again, not looking for any kind of real mischief. My mom had a small garden out there, full of vegetables she'd painstakingly nurtured. Baby carrots were my favorite. I loved pulling them fresh from the earth, washing them off with the garden hose, and eating them right there in the yard. They were the sweetest carrots I'd ever tasted, and I never gave a second thought to how much work my mom had put into growing them. At that age, I didn't really think about what belonged to whom, and I certainly didn't consider my mom's feelings when I plucked her prized vegetables.

As we munched on the stolen carrots, we spotted a group of kids playing in the alley behind our house. I should've known that karma would catch up to me for raiding my mom's garden, but instead of taking the hint, we let our boredom get the better of us. Our dad had warned us countless times never to use bad language, and we took that lesson seriously, but we weren't above teasing. In our young minds, teasing was harmless fun, and on that day, we decided to yell at the kids from the safety of our backyard.

"Hey, you guys are a bunch of tweety birds!" we shouted careful to use only non-explicit words, our hands cupped around our mouths for effect.

It wasn't clever, and it didn't make much sense, but we thought it was hilarious. At least we hadn't used any profanity. The kids in the alley, however, were not amused. They glared at us, confused and angry, even though they probably had no idea what we meant. It didn't matter, we'd gotten their attention, and that was all we wanted. We were sure we were safe on our own property, surely they wouldn't dare invade our land, but we were wrong. As they started to approach, climbing over the fence and squeezing through the gate, we realized our mistake.

"We're going to get you!" they yelled.

Ted and I, our confidence evaporating in an instant, ran for the house. We barely made it inside, slamming the door behind us and locking it, hearts pounding. Safe at last, or so we thought. A few moments later, there was a knock at the front door. We crept around the corner, peeking out to see who it was.

The boys from the alley stood there, faces red with anger. My dad answered the door, his usual calm demeanor stiffening when he saw them.

"Your sons were calling us fuckers and sons of bitches from the backyard," one of the boys said.

"Are you sure it was my sons?" my dad asked, his voice low and measured.

"Yes, it was them," another boy chimed in, pointing directly at Ted and me.

I watched as my dad thanked them, closing the door with a quiet finality that sent chills down my spine. The boys wore smug, victorious grins as they left, knowing they had the upper hand.

Without a word, my dad turned to us, his expression darker than I'd ever seen it. He led us upstairs, the silence between us heavy with dread. When he pulled off his thick leather belt, my stomach twisted. I knew what was coming. He turned me around, pushing me over the bed, and the spanking began. It was harder than usual, each strike burning into my skin. It went on and on, far longer than it ever had before. I clenched my teeth, willing the punishment to end, but it didn't. Time seemed to stretch endlessly. By the time it was over, I was numb, physically and emotionally. I watched through blurry eyes as Ted endured the same fate.

It was, at the time, the worst beating of our lives. What stung the most wasn't just the pain, it was that my dad hadn't asked for our side of the story. He had taken the word of the alley kids and punished us without question. My dad, the deeply religious man who believed he was doing the right thing, by putting the fear of God into us. But it wasn't God I feared from that day forward; I feared my dad.

That fear haunted me long after the bruises faded. Nightmares plagued me well into my twenties, dreams of my dad chasing me, his belt in hand, intent on hurting me. I woke from those night terrors in a cold sweat, my heart racing, still that scared little boy in the backyard. I had learned many lessons that fateful day. One of them was that teasing and taunting, no matter how harmless it seemed, could have real consequences. But the hardest lesson was that the person you fear most could be the one who's supposed to protect you.

Chapter 10

As a child, I had a passion for climbing. There was something about being small that gave me an edge, a sort of freedom others didn't seem to have. Trees were my usual go-to, but if I wasn't scaling branches, I was climbing door frames inside the house, defying the limits of what was "allowed." But it was when I was six that I made my most daring ascent yet.

The entrance to our attic was in the ceiling above our tallest stairwell, and I found a way to get there that felt like my own secret passage. With my hands pressed against one wall and my feet against the opposite, I could slowly push myself upwards, inch by inch. It wasn't quite climbing in the traditional sense, more like walking up the wall using all four of my limbs. At the time, I was just the right size, with just the right reach, and it gave me excellent leverage. Every time I made the ascent, I felt like a little spider scaling the narrow corridor, creeping toward my forbidden destination.

My mom was terrified every time she caught me mid-climb. I'd hear her shout from the bottom of the stairs, but by then, it was too late. Once I wriggled through the attic opening in the ceiling, I was out of her reach. It was hilarious to me at the time, someone who usually had absolute control over me was suddenly powerless. Looking back, I can't help but think maybe that's where my stubborn desire for control started, climbing higher and higher, beyond anyone's grasp.

Ted, my younger brother by just a year and a half, was always on my heels. Though younger in age, he was almost my size, thanks to a late birth that made him bigger and stronger in some ways. He loved proving he could keep up, that he was just as strong and capable as I was. My mom's panic only doubled when Ted began mimicking my climbs. Soon, the two of us were sneaking into the attic together, our private little hideaway above the world, just out of her reach.

It wasn't long before the attic became our unofficial clubhouse. We probably should've listened to my mom's warnings. I'm sure all that insulation wasn't doing our young lungs any favors, but we were unaware and didn't care. For us, it was liberating. Up there, in that dusty space beneath the roof, we could do anything we wanted, away from prying eyes. We'd spend hours exploring, ducking under beams and crawling through the uninhabited corners of the house, feeling like we had unlocked some secret world.

There were large vents on either side of the roof, and we would crouch there, peeking through the slats to watch the neighbors below, completely unseen. It was thrilling, spying on the world from above, our little kingdom. The simple pleasures of childhood were everything back then, climbing walls, sneaking into forbidden spaces, and feeling, for once, like we were little kings. Sometimes, I wish I could recapture that boundless energy, that sense of adventure. But in those moments, up in the attic with Ted, we didn't need anything more. We had our little secret world, and it was perfect.

* * *

Beside my parents' property stood a tall rock wall. To most, it was just a barrier, but to me, it was an irresistible challenge. I had always been the type of kid who sought out adventure, and that wall called to me like a mountain waiting to be conquered. So, one day, I decided to climb it. I scrambled up with ease, feeling invincible as I reached the summit without breaking a sweat.

It was only when I thought I was done, basking in the thrill of my small victory, that things went very wrong. A single misstep sent me off balance, and before I knew it, I was tumbling down. As I fell, time seemed to slow. My body twisted in midair, and then suddenly, I felt a sharp, searing pain. My armpit caught the jagged edge of a rock on the way down, slicing through my skin like a knife.

I hit the ground hard, gasping as the pain hit me all at once. Blood poured from the gaping wound in my armpit, soaking my shirt. I didn't need to look to know it was bad. I was bleeding fast. Panic set in, and I did the only thing I could think to do; I ran inside, clutching my arm, leaving a trail of red behind me.

My parents reacted quickly. My mom grabbed a clean rag and pressed it to the wound, telling me to keep my arm tight to my side to stop the bleeding. My dad kept his cool, but his eyes were full of concern as they rushed me to the hospital, the whole car ride tense with urgency. By the time we arrived, the clinic was minutes away from closing. The physician on duty was already halfway out the door, his jacket slung over his shoulder as he caught sight of us coming in.

He didn't look pleased. With a sigh, he reluctantly ushered us inside, clearly annoyed by the interruption to his evening plans. He examined my wound with barely a glance, muttering that there wasn't much he could do.

"Too jagged for stitches," he said dismissively, like he couldn't be bothered.

He didn't even wash his hands before prodding at the gash. I sat there, feeling the blood still trickling under his hasty touch, as he rummaged through a drawer for something. What he found was a single bandage and that's what he decided would fix me up. A flimsy bandaid slapped over a larger wound that was still bleeding.

"Good enough," he muttered, probably already thinking about getting home.

My mom's face turned pale with disbelief. She was horrified, not only by his lack of professionalism but by the hefty bill that came with the meager bandage. The whole scene felt like a nightmare.

When we got home, my dad took over. He had some military training in first aid, and it showed. He cleaned the wound properly, disinfected it, and bandaged it up with care. I could tell he was angry, angry at the doctor, at the situation, but he never said a word. His actions spoke for him, and I'm sure he saved me from a nasty infection that night.

It took a while for the wound to heal, and for some time, I stayed away from that rock wall and any other reckless climbs. But being the stubborn person I was, the call of adventure eventually won out. Before long, I was climbing again, just a little more cautious, but no less determined.

Chapter 11

When I was seven, my dad sold our house on Delridge and bought a new home on a sprawling acreage in Carnation, Washington. It felt like a leap into the unknown. In the midst of the move, my dad sent my mom, my siblings, and me to Oregon to stay with my maternal grandmother for a month. It was summer vacation, so school was a distant worry. To a seven-year-old, a month felt like an eternity. But it turned out to be one of the best summer vacations I ever had.

Every day, my cousins and I ran wild, playing from morning until dusk. We explored, made up games, and lived in our own little world of childhood fun. It was a summer of carefree days, the kind that you look back on with a nostalgic smile. But amidst the laughter and games, something happened that left a lasting mark on me.

My grandmother's neighbor, an elderly woman who lived alone since her husband had passed, suffered a stroke and died. The news shocked all of us kids to our very cores. Death was still an abstract concept to me back then, something I couldn’t fully grasp. But the idea of it had begun to scare me, more and more each day. I remember the sinking feeling in my stomach as I wondered, would this happen to me when I got old? Or could it happen even now?

It was the first time I started to dwell on death, something a child shouldn’t have to think about. My parents seemed so young back then, but to me, they were old. I laugh now, looking back at that temporal perspective. But at the time, the thought of losing them terrified me. A friend of mine had lost their dad, and I couldn't imagine how terrible it would be to experience something like that. I did my best to push the fear away, thinking that if I ignored it, it would somehow disappear. Of course, that's not how life works.

* * *

Just after my seventh birthday, everything changed. We had left the city behind, and my dad had finished moving us into our new home in the tiny town of Carnation. Growing up in Seattle, I had gotten used to the hustle and bustle of city life. The transition to the country was a shock. In the city, I could sneak out to a neighbor's house or walk to the local store. But in the country, sneaking out led to nowhere but endless miles of trees and animals. The nearest neighbors were distant, and soon, even they would become strangers.

At first, we got along well with the kids next door. But that wouldn't last. Within a few months, the boys started bullying me and my siblings. It wasn't just teasing, they made my life a living hell for years, until the day I graduated. With this change in circumstances with the neighbors, my only real chance for socializing outside my family disappeared. I was on my own.

The absolute isolation of country life hit me hard at first. I missed the city, missed the friends I used to have. My dog, Flex, became my best friend during that time. He was a chocolate lab, full of energy and love, always ready for an adventure. I didn't realize it then, but growing up without many human friends was shaping me in ways I wouldn't fully understand until much later.

I learned to rely on myself, to become self-sufficient. My parents didn't have many friends either, I noticed. Most of their friends were from church, but I always saw them as more like acquaintances. My parents never seemed to need a social life, and I guess that rubbed off on me. Without realizing it, I became a loner. I didn't mind it most days, but the lack of social interaction left me socially awkward, a challenge that would follow me into adulthood.

Over time, though, the country began to grow on me. I found a certain peace in the solitude, and my imagination kept me entertained. I spent hours exploring the vast woods behind our house. To a kid with an active imagination, the forest was an endless world of wonder. Every tree, every bush, every hidden animal felt like a new discovery. I spent entire days out there with Flex, memorizing every inch of the forest.

But the forest wasn't always a place of tranquility and comfort. There were times when I wandered too far and got lost. The fear would rise in my chest as I realized I didn't know which way to go. I was just a kid, alone in a vast, wild space that could swallow me whole. Somehow, I always found my way back, but those moments stayed with me.

By the end of the summer, I knew every rock, every tree, and every trail within a three-mile radius. Flex was always by my side, my loyal partner in adventure. When the end of that first summer in Carnation came, I had conquered the forest. I no longer feared it; I had made it my own. But just as I was growing comfortable, I began to crave something more. I needed a new adventure, something to push the boundaries of my world. And that adventure was about to find me. One that would change my life forever.

Chapter 12

Grade school started, and I was thrust into a new world, surrounded by unfamiliar faces in a strange environment. I had always struggled with talking to new people, making friends, and feeling confident in myself, especially when it came to my intelligence. I thought I was stupid, slower than everyone else. My dyslexia was the primary fuel for this sensation, making me feel like I'd never measure up.

Everything felt different at my new school. My old school was in the city, where I could easily walk to class. Here, I took a 45-minute bus ride each and every morning. And it wasn't just the long commute. The people here talked differently, dressed differently, and acted differently. It was hard to adjust. At first, I kept to myself. These kids weren't what I was used to. I tried to figure them out, to find where I fit in, but the longer I tried, the more I felt like I never would.

It didn't help that I was the smallest kid in my second-grade class. Being tiny came with its own set of problems. Worse yet, I was bored in most subjects and struggled to stay focused. Concepts like math came easily, but reading and writing? Those I avoided like the plague. I tried to survive school by paying attention to what the teacher said, relying on memory instead of the written word.

When the first test came, I started strong, but soon, the words on the page scrambled around in my head. Letters twisted and turned until I couldn't make sense of the questions. It was too much. Frustrated, I began guessing on the rest of the multiple-choice answers, not caring if they were right.

It didn't take long for my test scores to catch the teacher's attention. Within a month, I was pulled aside for additional testing in a special classroom. I guessed on those tests too, figuring it didn't matter. The result? They decided I wasn't ready for the second grade and sent me back to the first grade. I guess my luck with guessing had finally run out.

The humiliation was instant. My old classmates figured out quickly that I'd been held back. That's when the taunts began. They called me stupid, told me I was worthless. And I believed them. I had always felt lazy, too scared to try harder, and now I was paying the price. The constant put-downs only reinforced what I already believed to be true.

Being small, shy, and socially awkward in a new place made me an easy target. The insults came from all sides, and I wasn't strong enough to fight back. I wish I had been more secure, more confident, but instead, I began to spiral down a dark path of isolation and self-doubt.

As if the verbal abuse wasn't enough, some kids found new ways to hurt me. They mocked my clothes; outfits my dad had bought from Value Village. We didn't have the latest fashions, and it seemed like that alone was reason enough for them to gang up on me. Then, my dad lost his job, and things at home got even tougher. Our washing machine broke down, and my mom had to wash all our clothes by hand. An absolutely daunting task when there are six family members. She tried her best, but sometimes I went to school in dirty clothes, which only fueled the fire. The taunting grew worse, and the isolation I felt deepened.

Soon, the bullying escalated to physical beatings. There were bigger boys who seemed to take pleasure in punching and tormenting me whenever they could. My dad had made it clear that I wasn't allowed to fight back. He'd threatened to beat me if I did, and the memory of the "F-word" beating was still too fresh in my mind. I didn't want to experience that kind of pain again. So, I ran.

Luckily, being small had one advantage, I was fast. I may have been the smallest kid in my class, but when it came to running, there were only a couple of kids in the entire school who could keep up with me. Running for my life on a regular basis only sharpened those skills.

For a while, I felt safe, darting away from danger whenever I sensed it. But then the bullies started working together. They tried to corner me, to trap me where I couldn't escape. I quickly learned to stay on high alert, always keeping an escape route in mind. There were days when a dozen or more bullies chased me across the playground, but even with their overwhelming numbers, they couldn't catch me. I was quick, agile, and determined not to let them win.

Climbing became my other refuge. I had always been a good climber, and when the bullies got too close, I'd scale the chain-link fence or clamber up to the top of the baseball backstop. Once, I sat perched up there while they jeered from below, powerless to reach me. They gave up eventually, and I waited until it was safe to climb down.

This became my routine; run, climb, hide, repeat. It was exhausting, but it was survival. Every day felt like a battle, and I was fighting just to make it through. The loneliness of it all weighed on me, but I had no one to turn to, nowhere to escape except up into the trees or out into the fields. I thought the bullying would never end. But little did I know, life was about to throw even bigger challenges my way, and this was just the beginning.

Chapter 13

I had always known, deep down, that I wouldn't be able to outrun the bullies forever. When they finally caught up to me in the fourth grade, their anger was palpable. It was one of those days when trouble seemed to be brewing right from the start. That morning, our teacher, Mrs. Plummer, stood in front of the class with an unusually serious look on her face.

"Class, I have something important to talk to you about," she began. "I don't want to make a big deal out of this or point fingers, but someone took my calculator off my desk during recess. I don't care who it was, or why it happened, but I ask that it be returned by the end of the day. That's all I'll say."

Her voice was calm, but there was an edge to it. As she spoke, I glanced around the room, wondering if I could spot the guilty face. Who would take her calculator? As my eyes scanned the classroom, they locked with Jackie's. She was glaring at me, her expression sharp with accusation. Jackie had never liked me, and for reasons I couldn't understand, she always seemed to have it out for me.

Her lips moved silently, mouthing, "I know you did it."

I looked away, dismissing her stare and her false accusation. She can think what she wants, I told myself. I didn't take anything, and nothing she says will change that. But as the day wore on, I realized just how wrong I was.

At lunch recess, I was by myself, as usual. I was bouncing a red ball against the wall, lost in thought, when suddenly, I felt the presence of people behind me. Before I could react, someone grabbed my ball and threw it aside. I spun around, startled, only to find myself surrounded. A menacing group of kids had formed a circle around me, blocking every possible escape route. My heart started racing. It seemed like most of my classmates were there, and their energy told me one thing; they meant to hurt me.

Fear gripped me. I could feel it coursing through my veins, but it wasn't just mine. I had always had this strange ability to feel other people's emotions as if they were my own. At the time, I didn't understand it, but later I learned I was empathic. That day, though, the only thing I felt was fear, my own fear and the crowd's bloodthirsty desire to see me in pain.

The kids started shoving me, pushing me back and forth like a pinball bouncing around inside a machine. I recognized most of them, kids I sat next to in class, kids I passed in the hallways. Yet here they were, turning against me. As the shoving intensified, I noticed an opening in the circle. For a brief moment, hope surged through me, and I tried to make a break for it. But just as I did, Stan stepped into my path. Stan was the meanest bully in the fourth grade, a boy who seemed to radiate anger. I had heard a rumor once that he'd beaten someone up just for looking at him wrong.

Jackie stood next to him, her arms crossed, a smug smile on her face. I suddenly knew, without a doubt, that she had instigated this. She wanted to see me hurt, and she had gathered the perfect crowd to do her dirty work.

"Give us the calculator!" Jackie demanded, her voice sharp. "We know you have it. Your brother told us you have a gold calculator."

I blinked in confusion. What was she talking about? I did have a calculator, but it wasn't gold. Or was it? I couldn't even remember. The panic rising inside me made it hard to think straight. But it didn't matter what color my calculator was. They had already made up their minds, and they weren't going to let me leave without punishing me for something I didn't do.

The circle tightened, and Stan cracked his knuckles, stepping closer. His eyes were full of malice, and I knew I was about to get hurt. I felt trapped, my mind racing for a way out. Fight or flight kicked in, but I had no place to run. There was only one option left.

Without thinking, I kicked Stan as hard as I could, right in the groin. The larger boy let out a howl of pain and dropped to the ground, clutching himself. For a moment, I thought I might have a chance to escape, but instead, the crowd only grew more vicious. They shoved me harder, throwing insults and calling me names, their fury ignited by Stan's downfall.

Before I knew it, Stan was back on his feet, his face red with rage. This time, there was no hesitation. As I raised my arms to protect myself, he kicked me in the groin with all his strength. The pain exploded through me, and I collapsed, writhing on the ground, helpless. I braced myself for the next blow, certain I was about to be beaten to a pulp.

But then, through the haze of pain, I heard a voice shouting, and the mob scattered. A teacher had arrived, breaking up the crowd. She knelt next to me, asking if I was okay, but all I could do was curl up, clutching my stomach, trying to catch my breath. The next thing I knew, I was in the school office, and the secretary was calling my mom to come pick me up.

When my mom arrived, the principal told her what had happened, and she took me home to recover.

Every kid involved in the attack was called to the principal's office, but I don't think any of them got into any real trouble. I heard later that day, after I had left, the missing gold calculator mysteriously reappeared on Mrs. Plummer's desk. Only then did everyone realize I had nothing to do with it.

After that, something changed inside me. It had always been hard for me to trust people, but now it felt impossible. The idea that people could turn on me so quickly, over something I didn't even do, haunted me for years. I never understood why Jackie did what she did. Years later, I reached out to her on Facebook, hoping for some closure, but she claimed not to remember the incident at all.

I've never been good at letting go of the past. The pain, the fear, it all lingers. One of my biggest goals now is to forgive those who hurt me back then. It's not an easy task, but I'm working on it. Slowly, and diligently.

Chapter 14

One of the biggest struggles I faced growing up was my crippling lack of self-confidence. This lack of self-worth didn't extend to every part of my life. Despite my small size, I had always been athletic, and every year, our small grade school would test us on physical fitness. Depending on how well you performed, you could earn a special award, each one coming with its own coveted patch. The top prize was the President's Award, and I wanted it more than anything.

That year, our P.E. teacher had a surprise for us. She told us that anyone who earned the President's patch would receive it directly from none other than the current starting quarterback of the Seattle Seahawks, Jim Zorn. I nearly fell out of my seat when I heard this amazing news; Jim Zorn! He had always been the Seahawks' quarterback, and my family never missed a game. We'd gather around the TV every Sunday during the season to watch him play. To top it off, our teacher revealed that Jim was her brother. He'd agreed to come to our school as a favor to his little sister.

Football was my passion, and meeting Jim Zorn; that was like a dream. I wasn't big enough to play on a team, but I loved the game with every fiber of my being. The thought of shaking hands with him lit a fire inside me, and I decided right then and there that I was going to give this fitness test everything I had. No holding back.

We were given three attempts at each test, and our best score would count. Most of the tests didn't give me any trouble, I passed all of them at the highest level on my first try. I could run long distances at almost full speed, but sprinting; that was another story entirely. Ironically the sprint test was my downfall. I had gone in to the test way too confident, assuming I'd breeze through it just like the others. I'm certain I didn't put all of my effort into it. This would come back to bite me. When I crossed the finish line on my first attempt, I'd missed the time required for the President's patch by a second or two.

I was shocked. I couldn't believe it. I was fast; at least, I thought I was, and failing the sprint had never crossed my mind. Determined to make up for it. As I stood at the start line on my second attempt, my mind was still preoccupied with my previous failure. When the whistle went off, it took me by surprise. The hesitation may have cost me a valuable second or two. I pushed hard to make up for lost time, but again, I fell short.

I was so confused, running was one of my greatest skills. Now I was getting worried. I had one last chance, and if I didn't make it, I'd only qualify for the second-best patch. That wasn't good enough. Not when Jim Zorn would be standing there handing out the President's patches.

By the time my final attempt rolled around, adrenaline was coursing through me. The fear of failure gave me an edge, a focus I hadn't felt before. I wasn't going to miss it this time; no way. I was ready to run so fast that my legs might give out afterward. When the whistle blew, I sprinted with everything I had, pushing my body to its limit. I barely noticed my surroundings as I crossed the finish line. All I could think about was the outcome.

The moment of truth arrived, and I heard the teacher announce my time. I had made it. I had passed! Relief flooded through me, and the thrill of knowing I'd earned the President's patch sent a jolt of excitement through my whole body. I was going to shake Jim Zorn's hand!

The day of the awards ceremony finally came, and I could hardly sit still. They started handing out the second, third, and fourth-place patches. When my name was called for the second-place patch, my heart sank. I stared at the teacher in disbelief as she handed me the patch for second best. There had to be a mistake.

I walked up to her, my voice trembling with frustration. "I didn't earn this one. I earned the President's patch. I passed every test."

She looked at me skeptically but didn't argue right away. Instead, she checked her records, her face turning from doubt to surprise. "You're right," she said, her tone apologetic. "You did earn the President's patch. I'm so sorry."

She added my name to the list for the next presentation, and a few moments later, Jim Zorn himself walked out. The air in the room seemed to shift when he appeared. He towered over everyone, his presence commanding the attention of every student in the gym. Only about a dozen of us had earned the President's patch, and I could hardly believe I was among them.

When my name was called, I felt like I was floating. I walked up to Jim, my hands shaking, my heart pounding in my chest. He seemed even taller up close, a giant compared to my small frame. This was the first famous person I'd ever met, and I was so nervous I could hardly breathe.

He handed me the patch and extended his hand. "Good job," he said, his voice deep and steady.

It wasn't much, just two words. But to me, it felt like everything. I shook his hand, my own hand trembling, and for a moment, I was on top of the world. That handshake, that patch, it made the whole grueling process worth it. I was on cloud nine for the rest of the week.

When I got home, I tucked the patch away in my dresser, making sure it was safe. Every time I opened that drawer, I'd pause and remember what it felt like to earn it. Meeting Jim Zorn, shaking his hand, it was a moment I knew I would never forget. Even now, years later, that memory stays with me, a reminder of the day I pushed past my doubts and achieved something I never thought possible.

Chapter 15

That summer, everything seemed to unravel at once. It started with my Aunt Janice , who found herself in serious legal trouble. The situation was bad enough that she sent her three kids to live with us for a few months. Shar, who was eight, Mel, who was five, and little Fred, who was only two. It wasn't long before life took another sharp turn. Aunt Abey , facing her own domestic struggles, sent her two children to stay with us as well. Ned, the oldest, was ten, just a week younger than I, though several inches taller. His sister, Linda, was eight, with bright red hair like Ned.

Suddenly, the house was packed with cousins, and our quiet summer transformed into something altogether different. The days were chaotic and loud, but also full of adventure. We spent most of our time outdoors, exploring the woods, racing across fields, and finding ways to entertain ourselves. With so many kids, trouble seemed to follow naturally.

One afternoon, we were headed back up the hill to the house after a long day of playing. As we trudged along, Ned spotted a round paving stone lying on the ground. To him, it was a perfect toy. He thought it would be fun to roll it down the hill, and before anyone could stop him, he gave it a push.

The stone began to pick up speed, spinning faster and faster as it tumbled downhill. Kristen, my sister, was walking ahead of us, unaware of the danger heading her way. Just as she looked up, the stone struck her square in the face, right over her nose. I remember the moment vividly; her eyes wide with shock, the sound of the impact, and then the blood. So much blood.

Her nose was broken, and my parents rushed her inside, trying to calm her down as they worked to stop the bleeding. The rest of us stood there, shaken and horrified by what had happened. We were all angry at Ned. I don't think he meant to hurt her, but recklessness was part of his nature. He rarely thought about the consequences of his actions.

What bothered me the most wasn't just that he'd hurt Kristen, but that he didn't seem to care. While the rest of us were upset, worried about her, Ned remained strangely indifferent. He didn't apologize, didn't seem sorry. I knew his life had been hard; his father had been abusive, and it was the reason his mother was divorcing him. But still, his coldness left a bitter taste in my mouth.

It wasn't until years later that I began to understand Ned more. His rough childhood had left deep scars, and it seemed like he had never been able to heal from the pain. He was angry, restless, and often acted without thinking. It was as if he was trapped in a cycle, one that he couldn't break free from. The summer incident with Kristen was just one example of that recklessness, and over time, things only got worse for Ned.

Eventually, he ended up behind bars. It didn't surprise me when it happened, but it saddened me deeply. I had always hoped that he would find a way out of the darkness, but instead, he fell deeper into it. Even after getting out of prison, Ned slipped right back into the same habits that had led him there in the first place.

Sometimes, I think back to that summer and wonder if things could have turned out differently for him. If he had gotten the help he needed, maybe his life wouldn't have taken such a tragic path. I still pray for him, hoping that one day he'll find healing before it's too late. But the truth is, some wounds run so deep that they're hard to mend.

That summer remains a tangled memory of joy and pain, a time when we learned how fragile life could be. It was the season that left us with scars, some visible, like Kristen's broken nose, and others hidden deep inside, like Ned's wounds that never fully healed.

Chapter 16

That winter, the air was sharp and cold, and the pond had frozen over, tempting us with its smooth, glassy surface. Ted, Sean, and Ned, couldn't resist playing on the ice, despite how dangerously thin it seemed to me. I stood on the edge of the pond, my stomach churning with worry.

"Get off the ice!" I yelled.

Ned, ever the fearless one, turned to face me, a cocky grin on his face. "Why?"

"Because you'll fall in and die," I said bluntly, my voice rising with fear.

He laughed, dismissing my concern with a shrug. "This ice is plenty thick." To prove his point, he jumped up and down on it a few times. The ice groaned under his weight, but it held.

The three of them, Ted, Sean, and Ned, continued to skate and play, sliding across the fragile surface as if it were solid ground. I knew they weren't going to listen to me; they never did when Ned was leading the way. My concern only deepened, and I decided to show them just how thin the ice really was. Looking back, it was a terrible idea. I should have left well enough alone.

I scanned the area for something to break the ice with. There was a small log lying beside the pond, just the right size to make my point. I picked it up and carried it to a spot about fifty feet away from where the others were playing. I wanted to be far enough away that my actions wouldn't endanger them.

With a deep breath, I hefted the log above my head and slammed it down onto the ice. It broke through easily, leaving a jagged hole in its wake. The log bobbed in the cold water, an eerie reminder of the danger lurking just beneath the surface. I crouched down, carefully reaching toward the cracked edge, and pulled up a piece of ice, holding it up for the others to view.

"See? The ice is super thin," I said, pointing to the chunk in my hand, which was barely two inches thick.

Ned, predictably, wasn't impressed. He laughed and sauntered over to the spot where I had broken the ice, his breath fogging in the freezing air.

"What are you doing, Ned? Get away from there!" I shouted, panic creeping into my voice.

He ignored me, as usual, and reached for the floating log. The moment he lifted it, the ice beneath him cracked with a sharp, sickening sound. In an instant, Ned plunged through the surface, vanishing beneath the water. The ice shifted back into place above him, freezing over so quickly it was as if he had never been there at all.

"Ned!" I screamed, my heart pounding in my chest.

I knew, in that terrible moment, that he was gone. There was nothing I could do. I stood frozen, watching the smooth surface of the ice, praying for some sign of him. But there was nothing; no movement, no shadow beneath the ice. Just silence.

"Ned!" I called again, my voice desperate, but the pond remained still.

My legs felt like they were made of lead, my mind racing with panic and helplessness. Then, suddenly, a fist punched through the ice. It was Ned's hand, clawing its way back to the surface. He slammed his other hand down next to the first and, with a strength fueled by desperation, pulled himself out of the water. His clothes were soaked, and his body shook violently as he stumbled back onto the ice.

"It's cold, it’s cold," he muttered, his teeth chattering as he wrapped his arms around himself.

"Come on, Ned!" we shouted, rushing to his side.

We didn’t waste a second. Ted and I helped him off the ice, half-carrying, half-dragging him up the hill toward the house. My heart was still racing, but I couldn’t afford to panic now. Ned was freezing, and every second counted.

Inside, my mom quickly stripped him out of his wet clothes and put him into a hot bath. Slowly, the color returned to his cheeks, and the shivering soon subsided. Within an hour, he was back to his old self, full of mischief, laughing about the whole ordeal as if it had been some great adventure. But I couldn’t shake the guilt. If I hadn’t tried to prove my point, maybe none of this would have happened. I thought I was protecting them, showing them how dangerous the ice was. But instead, I had almost cost Ned his life. The weight of that realization settled over me like a heavy blanket.

I did learn another valuable lesson that day; be very careful of your actions. No matter how well intended, they can have lasting repercussions that may effect the ones you love. Hind sight is always twenty twenty. I had no idea at the time how blind I was to the dangers of my actions.

* * *

Eventually, the time came for my cousins to return home. As much as Ned's antics frustrated me at times, I was sad to see them all go. That summer and winter had been some of the most exciting months of my life. For the first time, I wasn't alone. I had people to talk to, to play with, and even get into trouble with. Despite everything, I missed them terribly. Ned was reckless, sure, but I couldn't help but admire his fearlessness. I just wished he could learn to think before he acted. I suppose he wasn't the only one who needed to learn that lesson. But for all his flaws, Ned was family, and no matter what happened, I loved him.

Those few months with my cousins will always be a part of me. We shared moments of joy, fear, and laughter; memories that would stick with me forever. Despite the near-tragedy on the ice, I wouldn't trade those times for anything. Love you guys.

Chapter 17

The summer of 1986 was one of the most unforgettable of my life. That year, my grandparents took me to Expo 86, the World's Fair held in Vancouver, British Columbia. I'd never been to anything like it before. It wasn't just any fair, it was huge, a sprawling world of rides, exhibits, and people from all over the globe. The entire experience felt like stepping into another world, one where imagination and innovation were on full display. Every corner had something new to see or try, and I soaked up every moment of it.

One of the most exciting parts of the trip was buying my very first 35mm camera. Back then, digital cameras were still years away, and the idea of capturing moments with film thrilled me. The camera felt sturdy and important in my hands, like a gateway to something special. With only about twenty photos per roll of film, I had to be careful, thoughtful with each shot; but I loved it. There was something almost magical about hearing the click of the shutter and knowing that somewhere on that film was a memory, waiting to be developed.

The fair had countless exhibits, but one stood out to me above all others; the Native American exhibit. It left an impression on me that would last a lifetime.

The exhibit began as we entered a dimly lit room with stadium-style seating, all arranged in a half-circle around a small, rustic set below. The stage was designed to look like the Old West, with a crackling campfire and an elderly Native American man sitting on a log beside it. The man was real, not an image or a projection, and the firelight danced over his weathered face as he sat in silence.

We all took our seats, and for a few moments, nothing happened. The man sat there, quiet and still, the fire popping occasionally in the silence. I remember feeling a sense of anticipation, wondering when the show would begin.

Then, without warning, the man started to chant in his native tongue. It was a deep, rhythmic sound, and I could feel it in my chest. He reached into a small pouch at his side, pulling out a handful of powder and sprinkling it over the fire. As he continued to chant, the fire flared up in a sudden, brilliant flash, making the entire audience gasp in amazement. I was transfixed.

The man repeated the motion, throwing more powder into the fire, and this time, something even more incredible happened. From the flames, figures began to take shape. It wasn't just a trick of the light, these shapes moved, danced, and shifted as if alive. They formed a series of scenes that unfolded like a story, telling a tale, one that captivated me completely. The flames seemed to conjure the spirits of the past, showing images of the Native American way of life, their struggles, their triumphs.

The man on the stage sat back, watching with us as the flames performed their magic. The fire seemed to have a life of its own, weaving through scenes so vividly that it felt like we were watching history come to life. I was mesmerized. I couldn't believe what I was seeing; it felt like real magic. Even now, I'm not sure how they created such an effect. There may have been glass between us and the stage, some trick of reflection, but whatever it was, it worked. I had never seen anything like it before, and I haven't since.

That exhibit wasn't the only one we visited during our whirlwind three-day adventure, but it's the one that stayed with me. We saw so many amazing things at Expo 86; each new exhibit bringing a fresh perspective on the world. But as those three days came to an end and my grandparents took me back home, I knew I would never forget the magic I had witnessed at the fair.

I was so excited to share the experience with my parents. As soon as I got home, I couldn't wait to develop the photos from my new camera, to show them the pictures I had taken of all the things I'd seen. Even though I knew the photos wouldn't capture the magic of that moment with the fire, they were my way of holding onto a piece of the fair, a piece of the incredible summer I had spent with my grandparents.

Looking back, I'm deeply grateful to them. They gave me experiences I never would have had otherwise. That summer at Expo 86 wasn't just about the fair, it was about the memories I made, the lessons I learned, and the time I spent with two people who always encouraged me to see the world in new and exciting ways.

Chapter 18

A couple of years passed, and though I had hoped that things might change for me, nothing really did. School was still a place of fear and dread, where the torment never seemed to stop. I prayed every day that the bullying would end, but it seemed that middle school only brought with it more of the same. A fresh wave of new bullies joined the ones from elementary school, making it feel like I was surrounded on all sides.

I'll never forget one day in gym class when a group of them decided to lock me inside one of those small half-sized lockers. The cramped space closed in around me, and I felt the cold metal press against my back as I pounded on the door, screaming for help. It wasn't until a teacher, startled by the noise, opened the locker and found me there that I was freed. He looked at me with shock in his eyes, surprised I had even fit in there, but instead of asking who had done it, he just assumed I'd been fooling around. Back then, bullying wasn't something teachers paid much attention to, or maybe they just didn't know how to handle it.

* * *

Months later, I was riding the bus home from school as usual, sitting alone because my two younger brothers, still in grade school, took a different bus. I had long since grown used to sitting by myself. The kids who lived in our neighborhood, kids who had once been friendly when we first moved to town, had joined the others in making my life a daily misery. I still don't know what I did to deserve it. Maybe it was nothing. Maybe it was just me.

The biggest bully in the neighborhood was a kid named Tom. He was huge, a towering figure in every sense, and Jack, another big kid, was his sidekick. Then there was Ron, Jack's younger brother, who was in my class. Ron wasn't as large as Tom or Jack, but he was bigger than me. He rarely started trouble on his own, but if his brother or Tom were getting rowdy, he'd usually join in.

That day, as the bus rumbled to our stop, I could feel Tom and Jack's eyes on me. Their energy was electric, crackling with mischief. I caught their gaze, and it was clear, they were up to no good. I wasn't going to be their victim, not today. I decided I would run as soon as we got off the bus. I always sat at the front, so I'd have a head start.

The moment the doors swung open, I dashed out and bolted toward home. It was a little over a quarter of a mile to our house, and I figured I could outrun them. I was fast, and I had determination on my side. As I reached the first bend in the road, I spotted a beaten path through the woods, a second route home. It was rougher terrain, but I knew those woods like the back of my hand. If I couldn't outrun them, I could always hide. Two options were better than one, I thought.

Without looking back, I darted into the woods and weaved through the trees. For a moment, I believed I had lost them. But just as I began to feel confident, I tripped, my foot caught on a tree root, and I went down hard. Pain shot through my ankle as I struggled to get up. My heart pounded in my chest as I glanced back. They were closer now, Tom, Jack, and Ron, all barreling through the underbrush. Panic surged through me, and I scrambled to my feet, ignoring the pain. But before I could get far, I felt a hand shove me from behind, and I tumbled to the ground again.

"Not so fast, BOAR," Tom sneered, standing over me.

That cruel nickname; Boar. It was their twisted way of turning my last name into something inhuman, something they could hunt and torment. They threw it around like a weapon, a way to dehumanize me. I felt like I was nothing more than a prize stag to them, a form of sport.

"Get up, BOAR," Tom ordered.

Jack echoed him, his voice dripping with mockery. "Yeah, get up, BOAR."

I looked up at them, then glanced at Ron, who stood a few feet back. He didn't seem as invested as the other two, but he wasn't going to stop them either.

"I can't," I said, wincing. "I twisted my ankle."

"Fine," Tom said, his voice full of false generosity.

He grabbed one of my arms, and Jack grabbed the other, hoisting me up. For a second, I thought maybe they were going to help me get home. Maybe, for once, they'd show some kindness; but no. As soon as I was standing, they started dragging me down the path. My stomach twisted with dread. Something was wrong. After a short distance, we reached a steep embankment at the edge of the woods. I looked down. It had to be at least fifteen feet down to the pavement below, and the drop was sharp. A terrible thought crossed my mind.

"Jump," Tom said, his voice cold and commanding.

"I can't," I stammered. "My ankle—"

"Then fly," Tom sneered, and before I could react, he shoved me off the hillside.

I fell, tumbling through the air, and hit the ground with a sickening thud. Pain exploded in my knee as I twisted awkwardly on the asphalt below. I cried out, but all I heard in return was their haunting laughter. They stood at the top of the hill, watching me writhe in pain before turning and walking away, their fun over for the day.

"Help!" I yelled, my voice cracking with desperation.

I didn't expect Tom or his friends to come back, no, I was hoping someone, anyone, might hear me. But we lived in the middle of nowhere, and my cries echoed uselessly into the trees. I was alone. For a while, I lay there, gasping in pain, trying to figure out what to do. My leg was too injured to stand. The house was a quarter mile away, mostly uphill, and there was no one around to help. In that moment, I realized I had only one option; I had to crawl.

So I did. I dragged myself along the ground, inch by inch, using my three good limbs. It felt like the longest crawl of my life, the asphalt scraping against my skin as I pulled myself forward, my leg screaming in agony. But eventually, after what felt like an eternity, I made it home.

My parents were horrified when they saw me. They called the police, but when the officers arrived, all they did was talk to the neighbor boys. Tom, Jack, and Ron played innocent, and the cops didn't take it seriously. They told them to leave me alone, and for a while, they did. But in the long run, it only made things worse.

That day marked the beginning of a new chapter in my life, one where I realized that I couldn't count on others to protect me. I had to find my own strength, my own way to survive. And though it was a long road, I would eventually learn to rise above the pain they tried to bury me under.

Chapter 19

Every day, Dad poured his energy into the five acres of land we called home. From dawn until dusk, he was out there chopping firewood, clearing brush, and building makeshift roads through the property. It was a never-ending cycle of labor, but he seemed to love it. Dead trees came down to make room for new ones, and each day the land became a little more like the vision he had in his mind.

One of the trees he had marked for removal stood just outside the kitchen window. It was a towering thing, its branches reaching up into the sky, casting long shadows over the house. That day, Dad grabbed his chainsaw, fired it up, and went to work. The roar of the saw echoed through the yard, and the smell of freshly cut wood filled the air. It wasn't long before the massive tree began to creak and groan, then crashed to the ground with a thunderous boom, shaking the earth beneath it.

Inside the house, Mom was washing dishes when she heard the terrifying sound. Startled, she dropped what she was doing and rushed to the window. What she saw made her heart stop. There, just outside, Dad lay still on the ground beneath the tree, his body pinned beneath its massive trunk. His eyes were closed, and he wasn't moving. Her stomach dropped. Panic gripped her as she flew out of the kitchen, sprinting through the front door, her heart racing.

"Allen!" she screamed, her voice filled with fear.

She reached him in seconds, dropping to her knees beside him, her hands hovering helplessly over his still body. His eyes remained closed, and for a moment, all she could think was that the worst had happened. She wanted to move him, to somehow lift the heavy trunk off his body, but she was afraid of making things worse. She screamed his name again, desperate for a response.

"Allen!"

Suddenly, she heard something; a sound so out of place in that moment, it made her freeze; laughter. Soft at first, but then it grew louder. She stared down at Dad, her heart still pounding, and saw his eyes open. He was grinning. Before she could fully comprehend what was happening, Dad pulled himself out from under the tree and stood up, brushing off his pants as if nothing had happened at all.

Mom blinked in disbelief, her fear quickly turning to a mix of shock and fury. She realized, in that instant, that he had staged the whole thing. The tree had fallen safely, and Dad, being the prankster that he was, had simply laid down beneath it, waiting for her to look out the window at just the right moment. She stood there, her breath still coming in short, sharp gasps, staring at him with wide eyes.

"Allen, you're unbelievable," she said, half laughing, half furious.

Dad just chuckled, his eyes twinkling with mischief. He loved a good joke, especially when it came at someone else's expense. Mom shook her head, half tempted to punch him but also relieved beyond words that he was okay. Still shaking her head, she turned and made her way back to the kitchen. Dad was notorious for his practical jokes, and she had gotten used to his antics over the years. Some of them were harmless; others were a bit more extreme, like this one. But Mom had always had a good sense of humor. She needed one, being married to a man like him.

This prank, though, left her rattled. As she picked up where she'd left off with the dishes, the adrenaline slowly fading, she couldn't help but think about how one of these days, his jokes might backfire on him. And in the end, that's exactly what happened. Dad kept up with his pranks for years, always managing to pull one over on family and friends, making them think he was hurt or in trouble. But there's only so many times you can cry wolf before the wolf really shows up. And when it did, nobody was laughing.

* * *

After a long day's work, my dad often treated himself to a well-earned snack. His favorite indulgence was a bag of barbecue chips. He could usually be found on the couch, contently snacking away while we all gathered around to watch TV. Of course, the four of us kids loved those chips too, and after asking, he'd usually let us have a few. But there was only one bag, and we were a hungry bunch, so if he shared, those chips would vanish in no time.

Dad worked hard to provide for the family, and sometimes all he wanted was to enjoy his snack without having to split it four ways. He quickly learned that if he shared, he'd barely get any of his own. So, every now and then, while we sat watching TV, we'd hear the unmistakable sound of him munching away. But when we looked for the bag of chips, it was nowhere to be seen.

"What are you eating, Dad?" we'd ask, curiosity getting the better of us.

With a completely straight face, he'd reply, "Oh, I'm just chewing on my tongue."

As kids, we weren't sure whether to believe him or not. After all, he'd always taught us the importance of honesty, and lying usually resulted in punishment. But something about the way he said it made us suspicious. Deep down, we knew it was a fib, but we wanted to believe him anyway.

Now, looking back, it's funny how those little moments, those playful white lies, stick in your memory and make you smile. Dad had a mischievous side, and though he didn't always want to share his chips, it wasn't out of selfishness. He deserved a small indulgence after all the hard work he put in, and I can't blame him for wanting to enjoy it in peace.

After all, while we spent our days playing outside, his accomplishments were far more exhausting. Those small, seemingly insignificant moments are what build a person's character, the honor, the humor, and even the little bits of mischief. I miss those days with my dad. He was a funny guy, and those memories of him sneaking a snack while trying to fool us make me appreciate him all the more.

Chapter 20

Later that year, my life took a turn I never saw coming. It all started in middle school gym class when the wrestling coach made an announcement that would change everything for me.

"Wrestling season's about to start. We need participants."

I wasn't sure what it was about wrestling that drew me in, but something about the sport called to me. Maybe it was the idea of being part of a team, of testing myself in a way I never had before. Whatever it was, I signed up that day without a second thought. From that moment on, I was committed. I stayed after school every day, never missed a single practice, and gave it my all. Some of the other wrestlers took a day or two off here and there, but not me. I wanted to be there every moment, soaking in everything I could. When the season finally started, we were all guaranteed at least one match at every meet, but for me, one match was never enough. I always wanted more.

Every chance I got, I asked the coach for extra matches. At some meets, I wrestled three or four times, even though I wasn't particularly good in my first year. My technique was raw, my strength wasn't quite there yet, but I had something that others didn't; determination. At the end of the season, I received an award. It wasn't for being the best wrestler or for winning the most matches. Instead, it was a plaque with an inscription that read; "The Wrestler Most Likely to Ask for Extra Matches."

It wasn't much, perhaps more of a joke than anything, but to me, it was a sign that I belonged. It was my first plaque, and I took it home with pride, setting it on top of the dresser I had built with my dad the year before. He'd cut the wood, showed me how to hammer and glue the pieces together, and we'd constructed it side by side. That dresser was my first big project, and it turned out well, though most of the credit went to my dad. Still, having that small plaque sitting on top of something I had helped create gave me a new sense of accomplishment.

Dad was always big on teaching me skills with tools. As an electrician, he knew how important those abilities would be later in life. But at that moment, that little plaque meant more than any construction project. It was one of the first things that ever made me feel proud of myself.

* * *

By the time I entered eighth grade, I was ready to take things further with wrestling. I made the varsity squad without much trouble and started to win more matches. I wasn't just on the team anymore, I was one of the better wrestlers. I pushed myself in every practice, eager to learn, and over time, my skills grew. Wrestling had become something I loved, and it gave me a confidence I'd never known before.

One afternoon, after practice, I waited for the activity bus to take me home. I was tired but satisfied with the day's work when I noticed a boy I didn't recognize approaching me. There was something in his eyes, a mean glint that I'd seen too many times before.

This wasn't just a random encounter. He was looking for trouble.

He was about my height but stockier, with broad shoulders that spoke of strength. He wasted no time, swinging a fist straight for my face. In the past, I might've been too scared or too slow to react, but not this time. Wrestling had given me more than just skills on the mat; it had given me a sense of control over my body that I never had before. I dodged his punch easily, surprised by how natural it felt.

Without hesitation, I shot in and tackled him, driving him to the ground. Before I knew it, I had him pinned beneath me, struggling helplessly. For the first time in my life, I was in control.

"Let me go!" he demanded, his voice filled with anger.

"I'll let you go if you leave me alone," I replied.

"Okay, just let me up."

I released him, thinking the fight was over, but as soon as he got to his feet, he swung again. I dodged it just as easily as the first and took him down once more, pinning him in the dirt. A crowd of kids had gathered around us now, watching the scuffle with eager eyes. His face flushed red with frustration, but he was no match for me. Wrestling had given me the upper hand.

"Let me go!" he yelled again, embarrassed.

"Are you done?" I asked.

"Yeah, I'm done."

I let him up, but he tried to strike me yet again. It was a cycle that felt like it would never end, but I wrestled him to the ground for a third time. This time, I held him there, refusing to let go.

"I'm not letting you up until you're really done," I told him.

He squirmed beneath me, frustrated and humiliated, but he knew he wasn't going to win. The fight had gone out of him, and I could tell he'd had enough.

"Let me go. I promise I'm done."

Just as I released him, a teacher's voice rang out from the edge of the crowd.

"What's going on here?" he called, pushing his way through the circle of onlookers.

The boy, quick to save face, threw his arm over my shoulder, flashing a nervous grin.

"Oh, we were just messing around. Right?" he said, looking at me for confirmation.

I stared back at him, disgusted but knowing there was no point in arguing. "Right," I muttered.

The teacher, satisfied that there was no real fight, walked away, and the crowd began to disperse. The boy left too, probably realizing he'd lose again if he tried anything. I hadn't thrown a single punch, but I hadn't needed to. Wrestling had been enough.

Something shifted in me that day. For the first time, I stood up for myself and won. It wasn't just about beating a bully, it was about feeling strong for once, feeling like I had control over my own life. It was a small victory, but it planted a seed in me, a sense of pride I hadn't felt in years. That seed would take time to grow, and it would be years before it truly bloomed. But that day, something had changed for the better.

Chapter 21

A few weeks after my first victory over a bully, my newfound sense of confidence was shattered once again. It happened during one of our class breaks, those ten-minute stretches we had to get from one class to the next. On this particular day, several bullies spotted me in the hallway. One bully was one thing, but several, each one bigger than me, was a different story.

As soon as I saw them, I knew they had singled me out, and I took off running. It was a little surprising that they even bothered with me, given how little time we had between classes. But bullies never seemed to care about logic. Their only goal was to make life miserable for someone else, and that day, I was their target.

Luckily, I had speed on my side. My legs carried me quickly around the perimeter of the school where the doors to each classroom lie. I soon put a sizable distance between myself and my pursuers. Once I was out of their sight, I ducked behind a large bush that lined the outside of the school building. I held my breath, hoping they would charge right past without noticing me. Seconds later, I heard the pounding of their feet as they rushed by, just as I had hoped. A brief moment of relief washed over me, and I was about to step out from my hiding place when a stern voice made me freeze.

"What are you doing screwing around outside my classroom?" a teacher's voice boomed from behind me.

Startled, I turned to see him standing in the doorway of his classroom, glaring at me with suspicion.

"I'm hiding from bullies," I said, pointing in the direction the boys had run off. "They're trying to beat me up."

He didn't seem to care.

"You kids think you can just interrupt my class whenever you want, huh?"

I blinked, confused. I hadn't even stepped inside his classroom, let alone interrupted it. But then I realized his door had been wide open, and my frantic escape must have caught his attention. He must've seen me darting around, hiding, and assumed I was just goofing off with the other kids.

"I wasn't interrupting anything," I protcsted.

But he wasn't interested in listening.

"I'm sick of you kids screwing around. Come with me," he snapped, grabbing me by the arm and pulling me into his classroom.

Before I could object, he dragged me to the front of the room and stood me in the corner like a small child. My face flushed with embarrassment as the students erupted into laughter. The teacher didn't stop them. Instead, he seemed to enjoy the spectacle.

"Now stand there and let everyone see you," he commanded.

The laughter from the students echoed around me. I could feel my heart racing, my face burning red with shame. The bell rang, signaling the end of the break period, but I was stuck in corner officially late for class. Finally, after what felt like an eternity, the teacher let me go. I rushed out of his classroom and hurried to my own. My teacher glanced up from his desk and shot me a look of disapproval. He made a note in his book, and I knew without asking that he had marked me as tardy. I didn't even bother trying to explain what had happened. After everything that had just occurred, I was too humiliated to speak. Besides, I had the sinking feeling that no one would believe me even if I did.

That day, the small confidence I had built up after standing up to the first bully crumbled. It wasn't just the bullies chasing me that had done it, it was the feeling of helplessness in the face of authority, the humiliation of being punished for something I hadn't done, and the laughter of my classmates that still echoed in my ears. It was as if the world had reminded me how small and powerless I still was. And once again, I felt like that scared, cornered kid I had always been.

Chapter 22

I have to admit, I pulled off some pretty crazy stunts in my youth, and one stood out above all of the others. It was freshman year of high school, and one evening my family and I were watching a movie that sparked some not-so-wise ideas in my head. It was the 1989 Batman movie, and seeing Michael Keaton as the Caped Crusader swooping off the edge of a building inspired me. I had to know; was what I saw on the screen possible in real life? Could a person really jump off a building and glide to safety?

My rational brain knew it was probably just movie magic, but my teenage mind refused to believe it. I had to test it for myself. We had an old, beaten-up tent stored in the garage, torn beyond repair, so I didn't feel bad about cutting it up for my experiment. I figured if I could create a cape with wings similar to Batman's, maybe I could glide, just like he did. I sewed pieces of PVC pipe into the top and bottom edges of the fabric to form a sort of rigid frame. It wasn't the most aerodynamic creation, but I figured it might just work.

I wasn't completely reckless, though. For my first test, I chose a small ledge in the yard. It was about four feet high, something I could easily jump from even without my "wings." So, I took the leap. The cape barely had time to catch any air before I hit the ground, but the descent did seem a little slower than usual. That slight success encouraged me to try something bigger.

Next, I needed a better jump site, something higher but still within reason. I found the perfect spot;

the garage roof. One side of the garage was embedded into a hill, so part of the roof was only about four feet off the ground. I climbed up and leaped from the roof, but again, the wings didn't have enough time to fully fill with air before I landed. It wasn't enough to prove or disprove my theory, but once again it felt like I had landed softer than normal.

Frustrated but determined, I climbed higher up the roof to a spot about ten feet off the ground. This time, when I jumped, the cape filled with air, and I felt a real difference. My descent slowed, and although I still hit the ground, the impact wasn't too bad. I was onto something. This Batman stunt could actually work! Encouraged by my small success, I decided to go for the big one, the very top of the garage roof, a full fifteen feet off the ground.

As I prepared to jump, Ted and Sean spotted me and came over to watch. They stood in the yard, eager to see me break something, no doubt.

Ted, always the instigator, egged me on, shouting, "Jump!" with that grin that said he was expecting a trip to the hospital.

I couldn't back down now. With the cape fluttering behind me, I leaped from the top of the roof hoping for the best. The wings caught the air perfectly, and I glided down to the ground in what felt like slow motion. I tucked and rolled upon landing, just like I'd seen in action movies, and I came up completely unharmed. I had done it, I had pulled off a Batman stunt! In my mind, the impossible had just been proven possible.

Ted, seeing my success, was suddenly filled with bravado. "If you can do it, I can too," he said, despite my warnings that he should start small like I had.

But Ted wasn't interested in working his way up. He wanted to go big right from the start. He had to prove he was better, a continuing battle we fought over the years. He ignored my advice, strapped on the cape, and climbed up to the second-story roof of our house, around twenty feet high. Sean and I watched with growing dread as Ted prepared to jump. He barely took any time to adjust the wings.

He just yelled, "Watch this!" and leaped off the roof.

The wings flapped, but Ted didn't have the technique. He crashed straight into the hard lawn, face-first. The sound of impact was sickening, and I rushed over, worried he might have broken something. He groaned, dazed, seeing stars. His face was covered in dirt and grass, and he was holding his head, clearly rattled. He stumbled to his feet, muttering about how much his head hurt, and ran inside, holding his face in pain.

Luckily, he wasn't seriously injured, just stunned and sore. It could've been a lot worse, though, and seeing him stumble off after that jump brought the whole ridiculous stunt into perspective. Looking back, it's a miracle I didn't break something, or worse, during my little experiment. I learned an important lesson that day; movie stunts are best left to the professionals, and no, you cannot actually fly like Batman, no matter how hard you try. So, if you're reading this, don't try it yourself. It was a bad idea then, and it's still a bad idea now. I got lucky, but I was playing with fire. Some stunts are better left to the big screen.

Chapter 23

My freshman year of high school was not off to a great start. At four foot eight and weighing just ninety-five pounds, I was the smallest kid in school, again. I'd grown used to being overlooked or picked on because of my size, but nothing could've prepared me for what was coming. One day, I made a mistake. A huge mistake. I stepped into enemy territory without realizing it; the senior hall. Worse yet, I entered their bathroom.

I didn't understand the unwritten rules of this high school at the time. No one told me what it meant to be on senior hall, but I was about to learn the hard way. That corridor wasn't just a hallway, it was sacred ground, ruled by the seniors with an iron fist. They laid claim to everything in it; the lockers, the benches, even the air. And most importantly, the bathroom. No underclassman dared set foot in there. But I didn't know that. I walked in, oblivious, just trying to make it through the day.

As soon as I entered the bathroom, I felt a shift in the air. It was too quiet. The kind of quiet that makes you realize something's wrong, but you can't quite put your finger on it. Before I had time to react, I heard the door burst open behind me. Several large seniors rushed in. They were bigger than any bully I'd ever encountered, practically men compared to me. I was still just a kid, and I felt it more than ever standing next to them.

The seniors surrounded me, grinning like wolves who had just cornered a lost lamb. I looked up at them, wide-eyed, trying to figure out what they were going to do. Their grins widened as they looked me over, sizing me up.

"He's too small," the biggest one said, his voice dripping with disdain. "No fun in it."

The others muttered in agreement, and to my utter disbelief, they all turned and left. They didn't touch me. Didn't shove me, didn't throw a single punch. They just…left.

I stood there for a second, stunned, and then I let out a long breath I hadn't realized I was holding. Relief washed over me, but it was clear I'd barely dodged a bullet. I made a silent vow to never set foot in that bathroom again. I wasn't going to tempt faint in the future, my luck was bound to run out.

* * *

Things started changing at school not long after that. We got a new vice-principal, and the entire building was put under construction. The halls became a maze of half-finished renovations, with sections closed off, and many classes were moved to portable classrooms scattered around the school grounds. Everything felt chaotic, like the school was being torn apart and rebuilt from scratch. With the chaos came an unexpected benefit; the destruction of senior hall.

Gone were the sacred corridors, the notorious senior bathroom, and most importantly, the senior bench. That bench, which had been like a throne to the seniors, had been planted firmly against the wall for as long as anyone could remember. It was the symbol of their dominance, where they sat and watched over their territory like kings. Losing the bench was a devastating blow to them.

The seniors wanted their bench back, of course, but too many parents had complained about bullying in senior hall over the years. With the new construction and the vice-principal cracking down, the bench never returned. The reign of terror that had once gripped the school, anchored by that bench, was over.

For the first time in a long while, I could walk the halls without feeling like prey. The seniors' power had been broken. The bathroom was just a bathroom now, not a battleground, and the senior bench was just a memory. The senior bench was silenced.

Chapter 24

That year, I signed up for a photography class as one of my electives, and it turned out to be one of the best decisions I made in high school. From the very first day, I was hooked. We were each issued a 35mm camera, and I must've gone through countless rolls of film. I took pictures of everything that sparked my interest; trees, shadows, street signs, my family, and especially my cat, Dancer. He was a gorgeous white cat, and his sleek fur made him a perfect subject.

But it wasn't just the act of taking pictures that drew me in; it was the entire process. There was something magical about developing film in the darkroom, with its eerie red light casting strange shadows over everything. My favorite part was dropping a freshly exposed sheet of photo paper into the developer solution. Slowly, as if by magic, the images would appear. It felt like watching memories come to life, suspended in those tiny silver grains.

Part of our final assignment was to put together an album, categorizing our best shots according to the class requirements. I filled my album with pictures of Dancer, family members, and snapshots from around town. One of the more difficult assignments required us to capture motion, a clear subject against a blurry background, something dynamic. After some brainstorming, I came up with the not-so-brilliant idea of photographing people while in mid-jump. I enlisted my siblings to help, figuring their leaps through the air would make for perfect shots.

At first, I had them jumping off small things; a bucket, a ledge near the carport, but none of these jumps were high enough to give me the dramatic blur I was after. I needed something bigger. I scanned the yard for something higher, something that would give me just enough time to snap the perfect picture. That's when I noticed the garage roof again. The same roof I'd jumped from with my Batman cape. It seemed harmless enough at the time. I convinced my sister, Kristen, to help out. She was always up for anything, and she didn't hesitate to climb up onto the roof. I was focused on setting up my camera, adjusting the lens, and making sure everything was ready for the shot. Kristen waited patiently for my signal.

"Now!" I called out.

Without hesitation, she leapt from the roof. But we hadn't considered one important detail, the roof was still wet from a recent rain. As Kristen pushed off, her foot slipped, and what should've been a graceful jump turned into a disastrous fall. I watched in horror as she lost control, hitting the ground hard. The thud was unmistakable, and the sound of the air leaving her lungs sent a chill through me.

I rushed to her side. "Are you okay?"

At first, she seemed like she might be fine, just a bit winded, but then we both saw it. Her right arm was bent in a grotesque "Z" shape just below her wrist. Both bones were broken.

"Oh my Gosh," I whispered, my stomach dropping. "I'll get help!"

I ran into the house, screaming for my parents. My dad came rushing out, quickly assessing the situation. Calm and collected, he used a cribbage board and an ace bandage to brace her arm. It was ingenious, really, and later at the hospital, the doctor even complimented him on the makeshift splint. They put Kristen's arm in a cast, and although she was in pain, she was incredibly tough about the whole thing.

I, on the other hand, was devastated. Kristen was my favorite person in the world, and I couldn't believe I had caused her so much pain. I'd been so caught up in getting the perfect shot, I hadn't even considered the danger. When you're young, you feel invincible, like nothing bad can happen to you or the people you love. That feeling disappeared for me that day.

But Kristen didn't hold a grudge. In her usual way, she brushed off the accident, never blaming me, even when she had every right to. I loved her more than anyone else, and the thought of her being hurt because of me was unbearable. I was just grateful she would heal. Still, it was a hard lesson. I learned that even though photography could capture life in a fleeting moment, there were some things, like the consequences of a bad decision, that couldn't be edited out of the frame.

Chapter 25

A few weeks later, during my leadership class, I found myself in a moment that would change how I saw myself for years. The girl who sat in front of me complained about the pain in her back and shoulders. She asked if I could rub her shoulders for a bit, and I, eager to help, agreed. I began to gently massage her shoulders, hoping to relieve the discomfort she was feeling.

The classroom buzzed around me, students talking and moving about, but I was focused on the task at hand, trying to be helpful. For a moment, it felt good to be seen as someone kind, someone who could help. Then, cutting through the noise, a voice I dreaded shattered the moment.

"Why are you letting Boar touch you?"

It was Dan; a bully who had been the bane of my existence since middle school. Every time I heard someone butcher my name, it was like a slap in the face, a constant reminder of how little I mattered to people like him. Dan's voice was thick with disdain, his eyes filled with that familiar malice.

The girl, suddenly uncomfortable, asked me to stop. My hands dropped away from her shoulders, and Dan flashed a wicked grin in my direction, a grin that told me everything I needed to know. He had done it again. Made me feel small, humiliated, and powerless.

Anger welled up inside me. I wanted so badly to march over and punch him right in the face, to make him feel just a fraction of the misery he'd put me through over the years. Dan was bigger than me, but not by much. I knew I could take him if it came down to a one-on-one fight. But Dan never was alone, he always had a pack of bullies with him, ready to jump in and swarm anyone who stood up to him.

Mr. Miyagi's words echoed in my mind; "One to one problem, yes. Five to one problem, too much to ask anyone." And besides, I had been raised to believe that fighting didn't solved anything. I clenched my fists beneath my desk, imagining how satisfying it would feel to knock that smug look off Dan's face. But I stayed put.

For years after, I replayed that moment in my mind, wondering what might have been if I'd just stood up for myself then and there. Maybe things would've been different. Maybe if I'd punched Dan, or even just told him off, I would have changed how people saw me, or at the very least, how I saw myself. I imagined the rush of satisfaction that would have surged through me, the sense of reclaiming my dignity.

But I didn't act. And the weight of my inaction settled on me like a stone. My self-esteem, already fragile, took another hit. I felt like I had let another opportunity slip through my fingers, another chance to prove to myself that I was more than the victim Dan and people like him made me out to be.

The consequences of not standing up, of not showing some self-confidence, were real. It gnawed at me for years, like an open wound that never quite healed. I feared that if I didn't learn to stand my ground, it would cost me everything. Not just in that classroom, but in life itself.

Chapter 26

It was around that time when I saw her for the first time. The most beautiful girl I had ever laid eyes on; Jackie. The moment I saw her, I was smitten. Her flowing light brown hair and blue eyes hypnotized me in every way. Before then, I had never really liked girls; not like this. But something about her changed that in an instant. For the first time, I found myself wanting to be someone's boyfriend; her boyfriend.

But every time I thought about talking to her, the voices of the bullies echoed in my head, taunting me, mocking my feelings for her before I even had the chance to express them. The last thing I wanted was to give them more ammunition, more reasons to tease me, to make my life even more miserable. Still, the thought of her lingered, gnawing at me, until one day, after months of agonizing over it, I finally built up the courage. But not enough to speak with her face to face, so I wrote her a note. Nothing fancy, just a few lines expressing how I felt. I left it on her seat before she arrived in class, then sat at my desk, heart pounding, waiting to see what would happen.

When Jackie picked up the note, she read it quietly. My eyes were glued to her, and I could barely breathe, hoping she'd like what I had written. But when she finished, she looked around the room, her gaze briefly meeting mine. And in that moment, I knew; she wasn't impressed. I could see it in her eyes, and my heart sank.

Later that day, her friend Amy confirmed my worst fears. "She isn't interested in you," Amy said, delivering the news like it was some kind of victory for her.

"Okay," I muttered, trying to act like it didn't matter.

To add insult to injury, Amy seemed pleased with herself, as if she enjoyed crushing my fragile feelings. My heart shattered into a million pieces. The pain I'd felt from the bullies was nothing compared to this. Still, I wasn't ready to give up. I rationalized that Jackie just didn't know me well enough yet. Maybe if I spent some time around her, she'd see me in a new light. So I started hanging around her whenever I could, making awkward attempts to talk to her. Each conversation was a struggle. I was shy, an introvert, and expressing myself was like pulling teeth, especially with someone I liked.

But as the weeks went by, it became painfully clear that Jackie didn't feel the same way. She made no secret of her interest in other boys, laughing and flirting with them while I stood on the sidelines, invisible. I took the hint, eventually giving up. I stopped talking to her, stopped trying. It hurt, but not as much as the constant rejection.

Then came a new emotion I had never felt before; jealousy. When Jackie started dating someone else, I felt this unfamiliar twist in my gut, like a sharp, burning pain that I couldn't shake; I hated it. I hated feeling so helpless, so powerless. I wanted a connection, a real emotional bond with someone. For a short while I decided relationships weren't worth the risk. The pain of rejection was too much for me to bear.

That decision led me down a darker path than I ever imagined. My inability to form solid connections with people filled me with a deep sense of hopelessness. That hopelessness spiraled into depression, a new low I hadn't experienced before. I felt rejected, stupid, worthless; convinced that I was unlovable.

And then, as if things couldn't get worse, they did. One day, my beloved cat, Dancer, went missing; vanished without a trace. Dancer was my beautiful white cat, my constant companion, and I was terrified that something terrible had happened to him. Out in the woods where we lived, it wasn't uncommon for coyotes to snatch up small animals.

The next day after school, the bus dropped off me and my brother, Ted, and my mom was waiting to walk us home. It wasn't unusual; she often walked with us to protect us from the neighborhood bullies. But as we made our way up the long driveway, we heard it; the sound of an animal in terrible pain. It was a small, pitiful cry coming from the brush. My heart sank.

We followed the sound, pushing through the undergrowth, and then we found him; Dancer. He was tied to a tree with a rope around his groin. His screams were like nothing I'd ever heard before, a horrifying, tortured cry that pierced the air. He was in so much pain that he thrashed and fought as we approached. The neighbor kids, the same bullies who had tormented me for years, hovered nearby, grinning like they'd just pulled off some grand prank.

"Can't believe you did that to your own cat," they jeered, their voices thick with mockery.

I knew it was them. I knew they were responsible. The way they watched us struggle to free Dancer, the way they laughed; it all screamed guilt. But I couldn't focus on them. I was too busy helping my mom try to free my poor cat. His testicles were swollen and discolored from the tightness of the rope. He fought us the entire time, thrashing and crying out in pain. After what felt like hours, we finally managed to get him loose.

But Dancer, terrified and hurt, bolted into the woods before I could stop him. And he never came back. I was devastated. I loved that cat more than anything, and I knew in my heart that he hadn't survived. The image of him tied to that tree, screaming in pain, haunted me for years. I wanted to hurt those boys, to make them pay for what they did. But they walked away laughing, leaving me standing there in my grief, helpless once again.

I went home and made a small memorial for Dancer. I placed my favorite photo of him on my bedroom wall and cried. The loss was unbearable. And though I never got proof of their involvement, rumors spread later that the boys had indeed tortured Dancer, spinning him around in the air by the groin in some sick game.

It was the kind of cruelty that made me feel something I hadn't felt before; an urge for revenge. If I had been the man I am today, I would have made them pay one way or another. But back then, I was too scared, too broken. All I could do was mourn my beloved cat and carry the weight of that pain for years to come.

Chapter 27

A few months later, just as I thought the weight of everything would crush me completely, a flicker of hope entered my life. A new girl came to school. She was beautiful, with a radiant presence that seemed to light up the room. Her name, I later learned, was Becky. With her silky dark hair and dark eyes, she seemed enchanting. Something stirred in me at the sight of her, something I hadn't felt in what seemed like forever; a spark of life, a glimmer of hope.

For a moment, I allowed myself to imagine what it would be like to talk to her, to maybe even get to know her. The bullies hadn't had a chance to fill her head with their venomous words yet. She was new, untainted by the cruel gossip that had followed me since middle school. I thought maybe, just maybe, I had a chance.

I smiled at her one day, but my heart sank when she looked away, pretending not to notice. It felt like the universe was mocking me. Still, I didn't give up hope; not yet. A few weeks later, in gym class, we were forced to endure a session on square dancing. I prayed harder than I ever had in my life, hoping, begging that somehow I'd be paired with Becky. God must have been listening that day because when the teacher called out the partners, Becky's name was announced alongside mine. My heart leaped in my chest. It felt like fate had finally smiled on me.

As the music started, I reached out to take her hand, anticipation bubbling up inside me. But just as quickly as my hopes had risen, they were dashed.

Becky took one look at me, wrinkled her nose, and walked away without a word. Refusing to dance with me; in front of everyone.

I stood there, paralyzed, as the music played on and the other students danced around me. It felt like the world had stopped, like I was trapped in some terrible dream I couldn't wake from. My heart, already fragile, shattered once again. This rejection felt worse than all the others combined, and I spiraled deeper into the dark pit I'd been teetering on the edge of for so long.

That day, I went home feeling more broken than I had ever been. The weight of the bullies, the rejection, the loneliness; it all came crashing down on me. I couldn't take it anymore. I wanted it to end; all of it. The pain, the isolation, the endless cycle of humiliation. I wanted to be free. An eerie numbness washed over me as I wandered through the house, searching for something, anything, that could help me escape the agony of my existence. I wasn't sure what I was looking for until I stumbled upon a bottle in one of the kitchen cupboards.

"POISON," it said in big, bold red letters across the label.

I read the warnings carefully; Fatal if ingested. Seek medical attention immediately. My heart pounded as I poured the poison into a glass and mixed it with water. I carried the cup into the living room, while my parents were outside, unaware of what I was about to do. Sitting on the couch, I stared at the glass in my hand, knowing that drinking it would finally free me from the pain. Without hesitating, I raised it to my lips and downed the entire contents in one gulp.

I lay back on the couch, waiting for the end to come. Minutes passed. Then more minutes. I expected darkness to overtake me, to feel the world slip away, but nothing happened. Confused, I sat up, still very much alive.

Frustration welled up inside me as I went back to the kitchen, reading the label again. It was supposed to work. It said it was deadly. Determined, I poured another glass of water, mixed more poison, and drank it down, returning to the couch to wait for the inevitable.

Again, nothing.

Anger burned in my chest. How could I fail, even at this? My thoughts were jumbled, but I was certain the poison wasn't doing what it was supposed to. In desperation, I grabbed the bottle and poured the entire contents into the cup. I drank it down, feeling the liquid burn in my throat as it went down. This time, surely, it would work.

I lay there for minutes, and then hours, patiently waiting. Waiting for the release I so desperately sought. But still, nothing happened. I sat up, utterly defeated; confused and angry. Was I immune to poison? How could something that promised death leave me sitting there, alive and still drowning in the same pain I had been trying to escape? Eventually, I gave up, slumping back into the couch, realizing that I couldn't even succeed in ending my own life.

Looking back on it now, I'm grateful that I failed. In that dark moment, I couldn't see beyond the overwhelming pain that consumed me. I couldn't see the possibility of life beyond the suffering. But I know now that suicide isn't a solution; it only transfers your pain to the people who love you, the people who would have done anything to help if they knew. For anyone who might be struggling, please, don't take the path I nearly did. Don't let the darkness fool you into thinking there's no other way out. Talk to someone, anyone. Life is too precious to throw away, no matter how hopeless things might feel. I know that now, and I'm so thankful I survived that day to understand it.

Chapter 28

Around that time, our pastor at church announced a camping trip they were organizing, and I was immediately captivated. I had never gone camping before, not beyond the confines of my backyard, and this felt like an opportunity too good to miss. I was eager to experience the wilderness, the adventure, and the camaraderie that came with it. However, when I approached my dad about going, he gave me a condition.

"You can go," he said, "but only if you pay for it yourself."

I didn't have much money, I rarely did, but the idea of going on this trip sparked something inside me; I was determined. For months, I'd been saving my allowance, dollar by dollar, and it was barely just enough. Paying for this trip would take nearly all of it, but I didn't care. The excitement overrode any hesitation. This camping trip would be worth it.

Inspired by my decision, my younger brother Ted decided he wanted to come too. We pulled out our savings, and together we planned our first real adventure. Then, at the last minute, Dad surprised us both. He offered to cover half of the cost.

"I just wanted to see how much you boys really wanted to go," he said, a sly smile on his face.

His unexpected contribution made all the difference. It meant I wouldn't have to drain all my hard-earned savings. I was grateful for his gesture, and

I think part of him wanted to make sure we didn't lose out on this experience.

The day finally arrived, and we set off with a group of kids and adults from church, ready for our first true camping trip. The campsite was nestled deep in the woods of the Wenatchee forest, and the air smelled of pine and fresh earth. It felt like another world, away from the usual worries of school and home life. Each night, the kids gathered in the biggest tent for some evening fun. The first time we piled in there, we weren't sure what to do. But as the sun set and the sky grew darker, someone suggested ghost stories.

The idea caught fire. We each took turns sharing the scariest stories we knew. Some were creepy urban legends we'd heard from friends or movies, while others were made up on the spot. As the stories stretched on and the tent was filled with nervous laughter and whispered anticipation, something unexpected happened.

During one of the scariest stories of the night, the window flap on the tent suddenly flew open from the outside. Instantly, all the girls inside let out a deafening scream, and a woman outside, who had simply been checking on us, dropped the flap just as quickly, startled by our reaction. For a second, there was utter chaos; screaming, gasps, and then lots of laughter. We all dissolved into giggles, the tension broken. The adults, however, were less than amused. They came storming in, forbidding us from telling any more ghost stories. But the moment was priceless. We still laughed about it later that night, our faces hurting from the fun.

* * *

On several nights during the trip, we played capture the flag. It was my favorite part of this grand adventure. The thrill of sneaking through the pitch-black woods, dodging between trees, my heart racing with excitement, was exhilarating. I remember darting past enemy lines, creeping through the darkness like a shadow, trying to outwit my friends. A few times, I even managed to grab the flag.

One night, we were in the middle of an intense game. The moon barely illuminated the woods, and I made my way to the other team's base, my eyes peeled for any movement. I spotted the flag, victory was within reach! But just as I darted forward, ready to snatch it, I was caught off guard. A chaperone, hiding in the bushes, leapt out and grabbed me.

He was strong, much stronger than me, and though I struggled to break free, his grip was unyielding. I twisted and turned, but he held firm. That was the end of my fun for the night. The others teased me as I was escorted back to our side, but I couldn't stop smiling. The adrenaline, the laughter, the sense of camaraderie, it was one of the best nights of my life.

By the end of the trip, I was exhausted, but my heart was full. I wished I could've gone on more adventures like that. The memories of those nights, ghost stories, laughter, and capture the flag, would stay with me forever. It was one of the rare times in my life where I felt free, happy, and part of something special.

Chapter 29

In the past, I had been indifferent when it came to schoolwork. I can vividly recall sitting in class, half-listening as the teacher quizzed the students on verbs, adjectives, and a range of other English concepts. Each time a question was asked, hands shot up eagerly around me, and I sat there, clueless. The realization hit me hard; I was falling behind. The distance between what my classmates understood and what I did felt like it was growing wider by the minute; it startled me. I knew if I didn't make a drastic change, soon, I'd be too far behind to ever catch up.

For as long as I could remember, reading had been a source of frustration. Words seemed to tangle themselves into incomprehensible knots whenever I tried to make sense of them. But something shifted that day. I decided that I couldn't allow myself to slip any further. It was time to take my studies seriously.

I threw myself into my school work, determined to close the gap. I began to focus intently in class, putting every ounce of effort into my tests. I disciplined myself to read every single word of my assignments, no matter how long it took. I still remember how much concentration it required at first. I had to force my brain to see the letters and words in the correct order, untangling them one by one. My progress was slow; painfully slow. But with time, my reading began to improve. The words started to make sense, and while I wasn't speeding through paragraphs like some of my peers, I was making steady progress.

It didn't take long for my hard work to start paying off. My grades turned around; suddenly, I was bringing home A's and B's. I had never seen grades like that on my report cards before. With each passing week, I felt my confidence growing. For the first time in a long time, I believed in my own intelligence. But despite this newfound confidence, I knew I had a long way to go.

* * *

Around that time, the next wrestling season began, and I was eager to join the high school team. I walked into practice full of excitement, but the moment I saw the other wrestlers, my stomach dropped. These guys looked like they belonged in a body-building competition. They were huge; muscled arms, ripped abs. I stood there, a scrawny freshman, staring up at what looked like grown men. Intimidation hit me like a freight train.

I was the smallest wrestler on the team; by far. I weighed less than 101 pounds, which was significant because that was the lowest weight class. Being the only wrestler in that class, I was automatically placed on the varsity team. There was no one to compete with for my spot. I should have felt lucky, but instead, it made me feel even more vulnerable.

One of my first matches was against the returning league and regional champion; a senior who had dominated for years. As I walked onto the mat, my legs felt like jelly. I could already see the outcome before the match even started. He took me down with ease, defeating me with no trouble. The outcome was no surprise to me, but the sting of defeat still cut deep.

A month later, I was scheduled to face another tough opponent, this time the returning runner-up. He was a junior and had only ever lost to the regional champion, the same guy who had already crushed me. I tried not to think about it too much, but dread gnawed at me. When we faced off, I knew it was going to be another long match. My goal wasn't even to win, it was just to lose as gracefully as possible. But once again, I was overpowered, and I walked off the mat with another loss weighing heavy on my shoulders.

I felt overwhelmed. Wrestling was turning into a battle I wasn't sure I could win. The competition was relentless, and I was struggling to keep up. The thought of quitting crossed my mind more than once. But something inside me refused to give up. I'd always been taught not to be a quitter, and though I was battered and bruised, both physically and emotionally, I kept going.

I didn't know if I had it in me to become a champion, but I knew I couldn't walk away from the fight; not yet.

Chapter 30

One cold afternoon, after wrestling practice, something felt off. My usual routine was to get picked up by my mom at the bottom of Tolt Hill, but this day was different; she wasn't there. The activity bus had dropped me off far from home, about four miles away, with most of the journey uphill. Normally, my mom would be waiting in her car, ready to spare me the long walk after a grueling practice, but today, the spot where she usually parked was empty.

At first, I wasn't too concerned. Mom could be forgetful, and it wouldn't have been the first time she'd gotten the pickup time wrong. But still, a strange feeling tugged at me; a knot of unease in the pit of my stomach that I couldn't shake. As I started up the hill, my frustration at the long walk battled with the growing sense that something wasn't right.

Then, I saw Ted.

He was riding down the hill on his bike, speeding towards me. He never came to get me after practice; not once. His appearance confirmed what my gut had been telling me, something was very wrong. As he neared, I saw the look on his face, and I knew that whatever he had to say, it wouldn't be good.

"Joe," Ted called out, his voice strained. "Dad's hurt. He's been in an accident."

My heart sank. "What happened?" I asked, breathless and dreading the answer.

"I don't know. Just that his legs are broken."

That was enough to send my mind spinning. The possibilities raced through my head as I began to run, Ted pedaling beside me. Tears welled up in our eyes as we sprinted up the hill toward home. We ran most of the way, fear fueling each step, neither of us saying much, too afraid of what we'd find when we got there. When we finally reached the house, it was empty. Not a soul in sight.

"Where is everyone?" I asked, my breath coming in ragged gasps.

"They're at the hospital," Ted replied, equally winded. "Dad's in surgery."

We stood there, the silence of the empty house pressing in on us. We had rushed all the way home, only to find ourselves waiting, waiting for news we had no control over. Sean and Kristen weren't home either, likely with Mom at the hospital. It was just Ted and me, staring at the empty space, our minds full of questions and dread. Hours passed, though it felt like days. When Mom finally walked through the door, her face drawn with worry, we hung on her every word.

"Your father's had an accident at work," she said, her voice heavy with the weight of the news. "He fell from a lift, twenty feet down, into a metal tool bin."

My heart clenched as I imagined the scene.

"His torso, arms, and head landed inside the bin," she continued, "but his legs didn't make it inside. The bin was too small. His thighs hit the edge, and broke at mid thigh. He's been through surgery, and they've put pins inside his legs."

"Is he going to be okay?" we asked, the question tumbling out in unison.

"He's doing better now," Mom reassured us. "The doctors say he'll make a full recovery, but he's going to be in a wheelchair for at least six to eight weeks."

Relief washed over me, but it was tinged with lingering anxiety. Dad was alive. He was going to recover. But I couldn't fully calm down until I saw him for myself.

* * *

The next day, we went to the hospital. Walking into the sterile room, my heart twisted at the sight of my father. The once strong, imposing man I had always known lay helpless in the hospital bed, his face bruised and cut from the accident. His eyes were swollen, recovering from the injuries caused by the shattered glass. Mom explained more details about the accident, how he had been installing a sixty-pound light fixture when it slipped. In trying to save it from crashing to the floor, he had been pulled from the lift, falling over twenty feet. The light had smashed into the side of the lift, sending shards of glass flying over him as he landed partially inside the bin. It was a miracle that he hadn't lost his sight, it was a miracle he wasn't hurt worse, it was a miracle he was still alive.

Seeing him in that condition broke something inside me. He had always been invincible in my eyes, and now, here he was, broken but alive. It was hard to watch him go through the slow, grueling recovery process. From the hospital bed to a special bed at home, then to a wheelchair, and finally, crutches. Each step took weeks, but he made it through. He even went back to work after about eight weeks. The doctors said his recovery was fast, but to me, it felt like an eternity.

Looking back now, I know how incredibly lucky we were. I can't even imagine what life would have been like if we had lost him at that point in my life.

Chapter 31

While in high school, I discovered a new passion; making home movies. With the help of my siblings and some kids from church, we recreated scenes from popular movies like *Robin Hood*, *The Terminator*, *The Rocketeer*, and *Indiana Jones*. It was a blast for all of us. We spent countless hours mimicking the scenes we'd seen in theaters or on TV, diving into the action, and improvising with whatever props we could get our hands on.

I didn't have my own camera back then, so I borrowed one from my school. My chemistry teacher entrusted me with the school's pricy recording device, a responsibility I didn't take lightly. Knowing full well that if something happened to that camera, I'd be on the hook to replace it. A cost far beyond what my teenage self could afford; I was extremely careful. Every shot, every move with that camera, I handled it as if it were made of glass.

Our makeshift movies were a hit among friends and family. Some received good reviews, while others were clearly a learning experience. My personal favorite was our version of *Robin Hood*, complete with a surprise cameo from *Rambo* himself, who met his match in a final showdown with Robin Hood. We even staged an "explosive" scene where Little Jack was taken out by a "grenade." We were proud of our special effects, which consisted of a small explosive device we'd rigged up. When the device went off, the blast echoed across the valley, and smoke filled the air. In hindsight, it was probably way too dangerous for a group of teenagers, but at the time, we thought we were being careful.

Minutes after the explosion, my dad stormed onto the scene, clearly worried something terrible had happened. He wasn't thrilled to hear about our "special effects" and was even less pleased that we hadn't asked for his permission first. I braced myself for some harsh punishment, grounding or worse, but much to my surprise, my dad didn't blow up at us. I think he was just relieved that no one was hurt and nothing was damaged.

With a look that said, "Don't do this again," he left without dishing out any consequences.

We packed up the equipment, figuring we had gotten off easy. But the relief didn't last long. While I was packing up the camera, something went horribly wrong. The camera stand I was adjusting suddenly released, and the expensive device plummeted to the ground. I watched in horror as it hit the dirt, breaking into what felt like a million pieces. My worst fear had just been realized. The camera was destroyed, completely beyond repair.

Panic surged through me. I knew I didn't have the money to replace it, and the thought of facing my teacher, or worse, my dad, was overwhelming. In desperation, I gathered every broken piece, placed the camera back into its case, and returned it to the school, pretending nothing had happened. It was a cowardly move, but I was scared out of my mind.

A few days later, my chemistry teacher discovered the camera's condition. He was furious, and rightfully so. He called my dad to explain what had happened, and I knew I was in deep trouble. I hadn't been spanked in years, but I was certain that the belt was coming out this time.

When my dad confronted me, though, something surprising happened. He didn't look angry. He just looked... disappointed. He didn't yell or threaten punishment. Instead, he calmly told me I'd have to work off the cost of the camera by doing chores around the house. I was stunned but relieved. My dad, who I had expected to come down on me with fury, had chosen compassion instead.

That day, I learned an important lesson; taking responsibility for your actions is always better than trying to hide from them. Facing the consequences, even when it's terrifying, is part of growing up. And my dad, who had every reason to be angry, showed me the kind of grace I'll never forget.

Chapter 32

Wrestling season continued during this time, and by the end of my freshman year, I had an okay record; 14 wins and 10 losses. But there was one match that haunted me. At the league tournament, I faced the runner-up to the regional champion again. I had lost to him before, and I went into the match convinced that I would lose again. I wrestled cautiously, too afraid to take risks. I saw opportunities to score, but each time, I hesitated, telling myself that he was too good, that I couldn't beat him.

When the match ended, I realized I had let him win. The score had been close, and if I had just gone for it, I might have beaten him. I was furious with myself. I had allowed fear to hold me back, and it cost me the match.

That night, as I replayed the match over and over in my head, I made a decision. Next year would be different. I wouldn't let fear control me anymore. I would train harder, push myself further, and when the time came, I would defeat him. No matter the cost.

* * *

The following wrestling season began with a sense of déjà vu. My very first match was against the same returning runner-up I had faced before, the one who had taken second place in the league tournament two years in a row. Now that the reigning champion had graduated, he was the favorite to take it all. But something in me had shifted since last season. I had a choice to make; was I going to let this guy take the championship without a fight, or was I finally going to claim it for myself?

I was tired of being the underdog, tired of being beaten and letting it happen; no more. This time, I wasn't just going to show up, I was going to fight. The fear that had once crippled me was gone, replaced by a fierce determination. It was my turn to win, and I wasn't going to let anyone take that from me.

The whistle blew, and before I knew it, I had taken him down in seconds. I wrestled like my life depended on it, dominating the entire match. My heart pounded with every move, every point earned. And when the final whistle blew, the ref raised my arm in victory. I had done it. I had defeated the wrestler who had once been my greatest fear. As my teammates and coach erupted into cheers, the realization hit me, I could win. I could be a champion.

That match changed everything. I had proven to myself that I wasn't a loser, that I didn't have to be afraid. But the season was far from over, and another challenge soon appeared on the horizon. His name was Doug, and he was undefeated that year. He had also beaten the runner-up I'd just conquered, and he was my next opponent.

We faced off in the middle of the season, and the match was intense. I fought him with everything I had. In the final seconds of the match, I glanced at the scoreboard, I was ahead by four points with only fifteen seconds left. Victory was within my grasp.

"I've got him," I thought. "No way he can win now."

But in those last few seconds, Doug pulled off his signature move; a "Granby roll." Before I knew what had happened, he had turned the tables and scored five points. The referee blew the whistle, signaling the end of the match. Doug had beaten me by one point. I walked off the mat, furious with myself. I had let up for just a moment, and that moment had cost me the match. I swore it would never happen again.

The season marched on, and I kept improving, driven by that loss. When the league championship finally arrived, I found myself facing Doug once again in the finals. This time it was for the championship itself. I wasn't going to leave any room for error, there would be no mercy. Every second of that match, I wrestled with everything I had, determined not to give him any chance to slip away. The match was close, both of us struggling for points, but I refused to let fear control me. In the end, I defeated Doug and earned my first league championship title.

A week later, we met again in the regional finals. Once more, I fought with everything I had, and once more, I walked away victorious, claiming my second championship. It was one of the first moments that I took great pride in and my dad and mom where there for me watching each match and cheering me on the entire way. After that, I realized something important; I could accomplish anything I set my mind to, as long as I wanted it badly enough.

That year, six of us on the team became league and regional champions. Our team took first place in both tournaments. It was an incredible season, one that filled me with a newfound sense of confidence.

Chapter 33

Off the mat, my life was changing too. After paying off the camera I had destroyed, I continued to work and saved up enough money to buy my very own VHS video camera. This piece of equipment was something new and exciting at the time. Digital cameras were barely on the market, and cell phones were still crude and expensive. No one in high school had one yet. My camera became my prized possession, and I continued to enlist my siblings to help me make home movies. We had a blast creating little films, and I even used some of them in class for extra credit. Before I knew it, I had stacks of VHS tapes filled with candid moments and memories.

One day, while filming, I followed Ted down to the basement, where our old German Shepherd, King, was lying on the concrete floor. King had been a part of our family for three years, a rescue dog we loved dearly, though he had a strange bald patch on his chest. Ted swore it was mange, and though we had treated it, King's fur never grew back. Ted crouched beside King, rubbing the spot in question.

"You see this? It's mange," Ted said to the camera. "It's very contagious."

Then, with a mischievous grin, he turned and reached out his hand toward me, threatening to touch me with his "contaminated" hand. I bolted, running around the house as Ted chased after me, laughing the entire time. It was just a joke, but that moment sparked something inside me. From then on, a mild case of germaphobia crept into my life. I started washing my hands more often and refused to share food or drinks with anyone, no matter who they were. Over the years, the fear of germs stuck with me, though it never spiraled out of control. Still, it haunted me, a constant, quiet companion I couldn't quite shake.

Ted, with his knack for mischief, had once again unknowingly triggered a phobia in me, one that still haunts me to this day. I doubt he intended for things to turn out this way, but looking back at how our relationship has evolved over the years, I'm not convinced he's too torn up about it either. That's just Ted, carefree, with little thought to the lasting impact of his jokes.

But this one stuck. And it stuck with me in a way I never imagined. It's funny how something so small, so seemingly insignificant, can worm its way into your mind and take root. A joke, a moment, and suddenly you're left with a lifelong battle. Yet, I know the responsibility lies with me. Ted may have lit the match, but I'm the one who's kept the flame burning.

Controlling these thoughts, these irrational fears, is my burden now. No one else can chase them away or lock them up. It's on me, and I've learned that if I ever want to truly conquer this, I'll need years of hard work, years of challenging the things that scare me most. It won't be easy, but it's the only way forward. In the end, the phobia is a battle between me and myself. And though I'm not there yet, I'm determined that one day I will be.

Chapter 34

As time progressed and I avoided the constant conflict with bullies, I found it easiest just to keep to myself at school. I ate lunch alone, rarely talked to anyone unless they spoke to me first, and had pulled so far away from others that I didn't know how to reach out. There was one exception, though, a girl named Brandy. I had liked her for years and had always thought she might like me too. One day, I gathered the courage to call her and ask her to be my girlfriend. Much to my surprise, she said yes.

Now a new problem had presented itself. I hadn't thought about the responsibilities that go alone with being someone's girlfriend. I hadn't considered what I should do if she said yes. Instead of celebrating or spending time with her, fear took over. I was terrified of what people would say if they saw us together, so I avoided her. We never held hands, never kissed. I'm sure she thought I wasn't interested, but that wasn't true; it was my own insecurities that held me back. Eventually, Brandy moved on to someone else, and I couldn't blame her. I had let fear rob me of my first possible relationship.

* * *

As high school progressed, I joined several sports teams, track, cross-country, and tennis, and earned varsity letters in each of them. In track, I ran the mile and two-mile races and discovered I had a knack for pole vaulting. Cross-country was grueling but rewarding, with every race a 5K challenge. In tennis, I played singles and doubles, enjoying the strategy and intensity of the game. Sports became my outlet, a place where I could channel my energy and grow in confidence.

These accomplishments marked a turning point for me. On the mat, in the classroom, and even behind the lens of my camera, I was learning that with enough determination and courage, I could overcome the fears that had held me back for so long. But I still had a long ways to go.

Chapter 35

That summer was brutal; hot, sticky, and relentless. To escape the heat, Ted and I found ourselves at the river more often than not, exploring its banks, moving up and down from McDonald Park in Carnation. One day, as we wandered along the river's edge, we stumbled upon a golf course that bordered the water. Watching the golfers was something new, and soon enough, it became our entertainment for the afternoon.

As we stood there, casually observing, one golfer wound up for a powerful swing. The ball soared through the air, curving toward us, and with a loud splash, it landed in the river just a few feet away. We could hear the man's frustrated voice clear across the fairway.

"Shit! That was my favorite ball."

Without much thought, Ted and I exchanged a look. We had our diving masks and fins on us, so why not? I dove in first, and before long, I surfaced with the ball held high, grinning at my small victory. The golfer spotted us and hurried over.

"Did you guys find my ball?" he asked, sounding both hopeful and annoyed.

I hesitated but then nodded. "Yeah, we got it."

He fished a dollar bill out of his pocket and held it up. "I'll buy it from you. That ball's my lucky one."

I handed it over, accepting the crumpled bill in return. As he walked off, relieved, Ted and I glanced at each other with a new idea brewing.

“Ted,” I said, “what if we collected all the golf balls we could find and sold them to the golfers?”

His face lit up with enthusiasm. “That’s genius!”

With that, we dove back into the water. For hours, we scoured the riverbed, gathering balls that had been lost over who knows how many years. By the time we were done, we had over a hundred golf balls neatly piled in the sand. We sorted them by brand and set up shop right there on the riverbank.

Some golfers ignored us, while others stopped to browse our makeshift inventory. A few even bought some. By the end of the day, we had made almost $70. For a couple of kids in the early '90s, that was more money than we’d ever dreamed of. It was the easiest cash we’d ever made, and we were hooked. That summer, we spent every opportunity we could scouring the river bottom for more balls, cleaning them, and selling them back to golfers. We were making a small fortune, at least until the golf course manager caught wind of our little operation and ran us off. I was crushed; there went our summer income.

But not all was lost. That same summer, my dad and I kayaked down the Snoqualmie River. My dad didn’t usually do much with us kids, so when he did, it felt special. That day, he was in rare form. We hit several small rapids along the way, just the right difficulty for beginners. I’ll never forget how hard I laughed watching him tip over into the cold water again and again, while I managed to stay upright the whole way. It was one of the best days I ever had with him, four hours of pure joy on the river.

Chapter 36

My junior year, I repeated my performance in wrestling, becoming one of the team captains. My confidence was growing with every match. After one late practice, a young sophomore girl approached me. She smiled at me, and I smiled back, unsure of what to do next. It was rare for a girl to show any interest in me, and I sat with her for over an hour, talking about nothing and everything.

Part of me knew she wanted me to kiss her. It was in the way she lingered, waiting, watching. But I was paralyzed by my fear of rejection. I still carried the weight of my past insecurities, and they rooted me to the spot. I couldn't make a move, and eventually, her patience ran out. She left, and I never saw her again. I had missed my chance at my first kiss; again. It wasn't the first time fear had robbed me of something I wanted, and it wouldn't be the last.

*   *   *

During my senior year, I was determined to win the state wrestling championship. To stay in shape, I joined the cross-country team. I worked hard, pushing myself until I became the second-fastest runner on the team. By the end of the season, I had qualified for the regional meet, something I was incredibly proud of. But then everything came crashing down.

The weekend before the district meet, my brothers, some guys from church, and I decided to play backyard football. I loved football, even though I wasn't big enough to play for the school team. This was my substitute. Sean, Ted, and I had played together for years, so we knew each other's moves by heart. Sean and I were on the same team, and when I gave him a look at the line of scrimmage, he knew exactly what I was going to do.

He hiked the ball, and I sprinted across the field. The ball sailed through the air, landing perfectly in my hands. I was wide open, and sure I was about to score a touchdown. But just as I reached the sideline, my foot found a hidden hole in the ground. My leg jammed awkwardly, and before I could recover, Ted and David piled onto my back to tackle me. I heard a loud snap; my knee buckling in ways it wasn't supposed to.

The pain was blinding. I collapsed, clutching my knee as Ted ran to get our dad. By the time he arrived, the back of my knee was already turning purple. The bruise spread fast, and I couldn't move my leg at all. The next day, my mom took me to the hospital, where the doctor gave me the worst possible news.

"Your sports days are over," he said flatly.

Tears welled up in my eyes. "No, there has to be something you can do."

He shook his head. "I can tell from the swelling and bruising that you've torn all four major ligaments. You'll be lucky if you can run again."

I couldn't believe it. My wrestling career, everything I'd worked so hard for, was over. My mom held me as I cried, but it didn't make the pain go away. A few weeks later, as the swelling subsided, the doctor scheduled me for surgery. In the meantime, I hobbled around on crutches, watching from the sidelines as my teammates practiced.

Weeks passed, and I was back in the doctor's office for a final checkup before surgery. To my surprise, after examining my knee, the doctor shook his head in disbelief.

"Your knee is fine," he said.

"What?" I asked, stunned.

"The swelling's gone, the bruising's gone, and your ligaments are intact."

I was in shock. Somehow, against all odds, my knee had made a full recovery.

With tears in my eyes, I thanked my mom, who smiled and said, "We've been praying for you, my son."

It was clear by the condition of my knee that my mother's prayers had been answered. The image of the large purple bruise that covered half of my leg haunted my mind. There was clearly significant damage to my knee, and yet here I was good as new. It was a true miracle, one I planned on taking advantage of with my first opportunity.

* * *

The next day, I handed my coach the doctor's note, and he couldn't believe it either. It felt like a miracle, and with renewed hope, I stepped back onto the mat, ready to chase that state championship dream.

Only two wrestlers in the entire history of my school had ever won the state championship, and I had been there to witness those historic matches. I was a sophomore then, making my own debut at the state championship. I didn't reach the finals, but placing eighth still felt like a victory. It was my first taste of what could be, and it left me hungry for more.

Chad was the first to win the title. He was a senior, and I remember the day vividly. Before his finals match, he shaved his head completely, leaving it smooth and pale. His white scalp gleamed under the bright lights of the Tacoma Dome, visible all the way up in the stands where I sat. I was captivated by his presence, his confidence, and the raw skill he brought to the mat. Chad wasn't just another wrestler; he was a leader, and I looked up to him with a kind of reverence. In that moment, watching him secure the win and claim the title, I knew I wanted to be just like him. I wanted that same glory.

Now, as a senior myself, I could almost taste it. I was determined to become the third wrestler in our school's history to win a state championship. Until this point, I had never had to worry about cutting weight. I was naturally small, always weighing in under the limit while my teammates were starving themselves to make weight. I would even go home and eat dinner before a match, showing up with a full stomach and still stepping on the scale comfortably under my class. But that year, things changed. I was no longer the undersized wrestler. Standing five-foot-eight and weighing 135 pounds, I knew if I wanted that state title, I'd have to make some sacrifices.

I convinced myself that cutting down to a lower weight class was the answer. If my teammates could do it, so could I. I set my sights on 122 pounds, two full weight classes below my normal weight. It wasn't going to be easy. I didn't have much fat to lose, but I was determined. I cut out almost everything; barely ate, drank minimal water, and pushed my body to its limit. Slowly but surely, I got there. By the time I hit

122, I felt drained, constantly weak and tired, but I told myself it was worth it.

For a while, it was. I competed and did well, despite the exhaustion that seemed to grip me. But then I ran into the kid from Tyee. The moment we faced off on the mat, something felt off . He didn't look right; his breathing was heavy, and he coughed repeatedly, even on me. It didn't take long to realize he was sick, and the match became a battle of endurance. To make matters worse I lost that day, and a few days later, I came down with one of the worst illnesses of my life.

The sickness sapped what little strength I had left. Even as weeks passed, I couldn't shake it. The timing couldn't have been worse. I had made it to the league tournament, still holding onto the dream of a state title, but my body wasn't cooperating. I was weak, still sick, but determined to compete. When I saw the Tyee kid again, I knew it was going to be a battle. The match was intense, both of us struggling, but I fought as hard as I could.

In the end, it came down to a close call. The referee made a questionable decision, one that still burns in my memory, and I lost the match. Just like that, my dream of being a state champion was crushed. I didn't even reclaim my league or regional titles. All the hard work, the starving, the sacrifice, it felt like it had been for nothing.

Looking back, I wish I had just stayed at my normal weight class. I know I would have performed better, stronger, and healthier. I may not have become a state champ, but I would have had a fighting chance. Instead, I had pushed my body too far, and it cost me everything I had worked for.

Chapter 37

Shortly after the wrestling season ended, a new reality set in. My high school years were winding down, and it was time to think about what came next. College? The military? Some other path entirely? The options weighed heavily on me, but nothing seemed as clear-cut as I hoped it would. My dad had gone into the Air Force right out of high school, and it had worked out well for him. He built a stable career, and part of me wondered if following in his footsteps might be the best choice for me too.

I considered college, but self-doubt crept in almost immediately. Some aspects of school had never been easy for me, especially with dyslexia constantly throwing hurdles in my way. I wasn't sure if I could handle the academic pressure. Would I even pass the classes? The fear of wasting time and money on a degree I felt sure I couldn't attain gnawed at me. I wasn't ready to gamble my future on something that felt so out of reach. So, I decided to enlist in the military.

I started talking to recruiters, and it quickly became clear who wanted me the most; the Navy. Their recruiter was relentless, reaching out to me more often than the others. He made it sound so simple.

"All I want is a guaranteed electronics job," I told him one afternoon.

That seemed like a fair request. My dad had worked in electronics, and I found the field fascinating. It felt like a natural fit for me.

"Oh yeah, no problem," the recruiter assured me, flashing a smile that seemed a little too confident. "With your ASVAB scores, you can get any job you want."

I was a bit surprised. I hadn't realized my test scores were that good, but I was happy to hear it. As for the physical aspect, I was already in great shape from wrestling, so that part didn't worry me at all.

"OK," I said, "what's next?"

"You'll need to go through a routine physical examination. Just show up to this room on the date we give you, and we'll handle the rest."

It sounded easy enough, so I agreed, shaking his hand before leaving. But when I arrived for the exam, it was anything but routine. The process lasted six grueling hours. We were herded through like cattle, dozens of us, taking test after test. There was the colorblindness test, STD screenings, even a check for hemorrhoids. Some of it was humiliating, all of it exhausting. By the end of the day, I felt mentally drained. But I passed, and that was all that mattered.

A few days later, I had another meeting with the recruiter. This was the moment I'd been waiting for, the day I'd sign my contract and officially start my journey into the Navy. As I sat down to review the paperwork, I noticed something was missing. There was no mention of the electronics school or any guarantee for the job I had requested. I reread the contract, thinking I had just missed it. But it wasn't there.

"I don't see a guarantee for my school in this contract," I said, my voice tinged with suspicion.

"Don't worry about that," the recruiter said, waving off my concerns. "With your scores, you're guaranteed to get the electronics job. It's just not written here, but you'll be fine."

My gut told me something was wrong. "I'd like it in writing just the same," I insisted, pushing the contract back across the table.

He paused, clearly not expecting me to push back. "Let me check your scores again."

I frowned. Hadn't he already told me I was qualified? He knew my scores; this felt like stalling. A few minutes later, he came back with a different story.

"I'm afraid you missed the required score by five points. I can't give you the guarantee."

My frustration boiled over. "One of the guys I met during the physical exam said recruiters can waive up to ten points for certain jobs."

The recruiter shifted uncomfortably in his chair. "That's true in some cases, but not for yours."

I'd had enough. "Thanks for your time, but I'm not signing anything without a guarantee," I said, standing up.

I walked out, my mom by my side, and felt a strange sense of relief. It was disappointing, but I knew I had made the right choice. I had learned an important lesson; once you sign, the government owns you, and all your choices vanish.

A few days later, I received another phone call.

"Hello?" I said, lifting the receiver to my ear.

"May I speak to Joe?"

"Speaking."

"My name is Staff Sergeant Smith with the Marine Corps. I wanted to touch base with you and see if you're interested in joining."

I groaned inwardly. "Not really."

He was persistent. "May I ask why?"

"I'm not exactly thrilled with recruiters right now," I said flatly.

"What happened?"

I explained the ordeal with the Navy; the long physical exam, the bait-and-switch with my scores, and the lack of a guaranteed job.

"Let me check your scores real quick," Sergeant Smith said.

I had heard this story before, so I wasn't holding my breath. I wasn't falling for that again. The sound of shuffling papers permeated on the other end of the line.

"Looks like we can get you any job you want."

Ever skeptical I said, "If you can put it in writing, I'll sign. If not, don't waste my time."

He didn't miss a beat. "I'll get you that guarantee. How about I pick you up tomorrow at 4 p.m.?"

* * *

The next day, true to his word, Sergeant Smith arrived in his Marine service alpha uniform, looking sharp. He drove me to his office, and there it was; the contract with my electronics school guaranteed in bold black and white. I signed, joining the Marine Corps' delayed enlistment program.

Twice a month, I attended classes at the recruitment center. We trained for the physical fitness test, which required twenty pull-ups, 120 sit-ups in two minutes, and a three-mile run under eighteen minutes to score a perfect 300. It wasn't much of a challenge; wrestling practice had been harder. I soon realized I was the only one getting perfect scores, which surprised me, given there were about twenty recruits. Surely someone else could get a perfect score, but I was the only one in my group.

The Marines also taught us the basics of rifle handling. I'd never held a gun before, so it was both daunting and exhilarating. As the days ticked by, the reality of my new path settled in. Bootcamp was scheduled for one month after graduation, and I knew my life was about to change forever.

Chapter 38

The school year was winding down, and the long-anticipated Senior Day had finally arrived. It felt like a breath of fresh air. There were no regular classes, no homework, just a day of fun out on the track field. The whole senior class buzzed with excitement, hopping from one activity to another. It was the kind of carefree day we hadn't had in years.

I spent the morning making my way through all the events, hitting a baseball here, trying my hand at a few races there. But the one thing that caught my eye more than anything else was the dunk tank. It wasn't the tank itself that held my attention, but the person climbing inside. It was Mrs. Kimble, my old geometry teacher, now sitting on the platform, looking out at the crowd with a playful smile.

I had been one of her top students sophomore year, and if I was being honest with myself, I had a little crush on her back then. That probably had something to do with why I was so eager to dunk her now. The second I saw her climb into the tank, I rushed over, determined to be the first in line. But by the time I got there, two people had already beaten me to it. I tried not to let it get me down, I still wanted a chance, even if I wasn't the first.

For a dollar, you got six tries. Much to my surprise and delight, twelve throws went by without a single hit, and Mrs. Kimble was still dry, sitting there as smug as ever. When my turn came, I grabbed the six balls, one after the other. As I held the first one, I waved cheekily at her.

She wasn't worried. The others had missed, and she had no reason to think I'd be any different. But I had a good arm and a little extra motivation. My first ball hit the bullseye perfectly, and the trapdoor opened beneath her. She plunged into the cold water, gasping in surprise.

I couldn't help but grin as she resurfaced, dripping and wide-eyed. One down, five more throws to go. I dunked her again. And again. I hit the target five times in a row, each one earning a bigger reaction from the crowd. By the last throw, she looked more surprised that I missed than anything else. I laughed along with everyone else, satisfied that I'd soaked my favorite teacher five out of six times.

Later that day, as the festivities continued, I was wandering across the field when I ran into Chad. We weren't exactly friends, but we'd never had any problems either. So when he suddenly started shoving me, I was caught off guard.

I wasn't in the mood for it, though. I'd spent years letting people push me around, but that was over. I was going to be a Marine soon, and it felt like I needed to start standing up for myself. So, without thinking twice, I grabbed Chad and wrestled him to the ground.

It wasn't even a contest; I pinned him down in one of my best wrestling moves, quick and clean. Chad struggled beneath me, but he wasn't getting out of it. I held him there for a few seconds, just long enough to prove my point, then let him go.

Unbeknownst to me, someone had been recording the whole thing, and later the impromptu wrestling match made its way onto our senior video. Chad never really lived it down. People teased him about it for the rest of the year. But for me, it was more than just a moment of victory. It was the first time I realized I didn't have to let people push me around anymore.

* * *

The day of my high school graduation felt surreal. I stood among my classmates, tossing caps in the air, shaking hands, and exchanging hugs. It was supposed to be a moment of celebration, but truthfully, I barely knew any of them. Four years of passing by one another in hallways, sharing the occasional class, and yet, as we said our goodbyes, it felt like I was saying farewell to strangers. All of those years of keeping to myself isolated me from knowing any of them very well.

I watched as my classmates excitedly boarded the bus headed for the senior graduation party. It was one of the final events designed to bring us together before we all went our separate ways. But I wasn't joining them. I couldn't afford the ticket. So, while they piled onto the bus with laughter and excitement, I stood on the sidelines, pretending it didn't matter. My family was waiting for me, and after a few last waves, I left with them.

That night, I went home and tried not to think about what I was missing. The sounds of celebration and fun lingered in my mind, as if carried by the evening breeze. Later, when I saw the senior video, my suspicions were confirmed; they had a great time. I watched footage of the party, scenes of my classmates laughing, dancing, and enjoying what seemed like an unforgettable night. They even had a magician. I'd never seen a real magician perform live before. I remember watching, fascinated, wishing I could've been there. It seemed like such a magical experience.

Looking back on it now, it's almost funny how disappointed I felt. Who knew that high school graduation parties would one day become one of my biggest sources of income. Years later, I found my true passion and became a magician myself, performing for events just like the one I had missed.

In an ironic twist of fate, I even got to perform at Mt. Si's graduation party one year. I stood there on stage, watching the faces of the new graduates light up with wonder and amazement, just as mine had watching that video so many years ago. Only this time, I wasn't missing out. I was the one creating the magic.

Chapter 39

Bootcamp was looming just a few weeks away, it's shadow growing larger with each passing day. But before the grueling weeks of basic training began, my grandmother gifted me and Ted an escape; a trip to Disneyland. It was a graduation present for both of us, though Ted received his a year early so he could come along and keep me company. I'd never flown before, so when I boarded that plane, my heart raced with a blend of excitement and nerves. The flight itself was thrilling.

We arrived at the hotel in one piece, our bags slung over our shoulders, and after a quick drop-off, we headed straight for Disneyland. I'd never been there before, and it was everything I imagined and more. The rides, the colors, the laughter; it was like walking into a dream. The lines were long, but we didn't care. We tried to hit as many rides as possible, doing our best to see everything we could in that magical place.

The next day was just as exhilarating. We visited Knott's Berry Farm and Universal Studios, and by the end of it, we were exhausted but full of memories. It was our final day, and with the parks behind us, we decided to check out an arcade just down the street from the hotel. Ted, as usual, was taking his sweet time getting ready, so I told him I'd go ahead and meet him there.

The sidewalk buzzed with the energy of the city, so much bigger and louder than the quiet, familiar forest back home. As I walked, I felt a strange sensation, like someone's attention was fixed on me.

The hairs on my neck prickled as I glanced around, spotting a tall, stalky man approaching me from the other direction. He looked Hispanic, over six feet tall and easily two hundred pounds. His presence made me uneasy, though I couldn't explain why.

I was only eighteen, but my small frame and boyish face made me look much younger. Five-foot-eight, 135 pounds. To this man, I must've seemed like a kid. Something then happened that I still to this day can't fully explain. As we passed each other on the sidewalk, and though he didn't say a word or make a move directly toward me, something unbelievable happened. It was like a shadow leaped out from him, not something I could see with my eyes, but something I could feel; a dark, suffocating presence reaching for me. It tried to attack me or grab me, but as it surrounded me it disappeared like mist in the wind.

I jumped back, startled, as he continued walking by. Trying not to appear rattled, I kept moving forward, but I couldn't shake the sense that something was very wrong. A few steps later, I glanced over my shoulder. The man had turned around and was staring at me. My pulse quickened. I sped up, trying to get some distance between us, but when I looked back again, he was following me.

My heart raced, and I broke into a full sprint. I'd always been fast; wrestling had kept me in great shape, and I was confident this guy couldn't keep up. I ran several blocks without stopping, darting into the arcade and feeling a wave of relief wash over me. Surely, I was safe now. He was long gone and there was no way he had been able to keep up with me.

Inside, I played a few games, the bright lights and cheerful noises helping me shake off the eerie feeling. But just when I thought I was safe, the sensation returned. I felt the eerie presence again, like a cold hand hovering over my shoulder. I turned slowly, and there he was, standing just a few feet away, watching me. My hands trembled, and the game became impossible to play. I died in the game within seconds, but before I could move, the man leaned in and placed a coin in the slot.

"I'm no good at these games," he said in a low, gruff voice. "You go ahead and play."

"Thanks," I mumbled, trying to keep my voice steady. My hands shook so badly that I lost in the game again almost immediately.

I stepped away from the machine, frantically searching for Ted. When I found him, I rushed over. He was engrossed in a game, completely oblivious.

"Ted, there's a guy who's been following me. I think he wants to kill me," I whispered, my voice tight with fear.

"What?" He barely glanced up from his screen.

I pointed toward the man, who quickly looked away as soon as Ted turned in his direction.

"That guy’s been watching me this whole time."

After glancing at the man, Ted shrugged. "You're being paranoid," he said, turning back to his game. "Stop distracting me."

Frustrated, I tried to focus on the games, but it was impossible to shake the feeling that the man was still lurking in the background, his eyes on me. Hours passed, and by the time the arcade was ready to close, only a few people remained, me, Ted, the manager, and that man.

Ted, arms full of tickets, headed to the counter to cash them in. I helped him, my anxiety growing with every minute that passed.

"Ted, that guy's still here. He's been watching me the whole time."

"You're imagining things," Ted muttered.

The manager overheard this time. "What guy?" he asked.

I pointed at the man standing near the south entrance. The manager's expression darkened as he followed my finger, his eyes narrowing.

"Alright," the manager said calmly. "I want you two to leave through the north exit. Act normal, don't look at him. I'll watch to see what he does."

Ted and I walked out as casually as we could, taking a dozen steps before a sharp whistle pierced the air. We turned to see the manager frantically motioning for us to come back inside. We rushed back, and he quickly locked the door behind us. Seconds later, the dark sinister man rounded the corner, his eyes wild as he yanked on the locked door.

"You were right about him," the manager said. "The second you two left, he tried to follow out the south entrance."

Ted finally looked at me, the realization settling in.

"I told you," I muttered, feeling a mix of vindication and lingering fear.

The manager gave us some extra tokens and let us play a few more games while he finished closing up the arcade. When he was done, he offered to drive us back to the hotel. We gratefully accepted. That night, I couldn't shake the feeling that the manager had saved our lives. I wish I could have thanked him more. Sometimes when all hope has faded, the universe finds ways to put just the right person in just the right place to make a difference in your life. This was clearly the case with this man.

Chapter 40

A few days after my nineteenth birthday the time had finally arrived, and it was time for me to head off to Marine boot camp. I wasn't afraid as I boarded the plane bound for California, not even when I stepped onto the bus to the training facility. But that changed the moment I got off the bus and heard the voice of my senior drill instructor for the first time. It wasn't just a voice; it was a thunderous roar that struck fear deep into my core. I had never heard anyone yell with such intensity, and it made my heart race.

The senior drill instructor wasn't alone. Several other drill instructors surrounded us, screaming in our faces, barking orders, demanding that we stand on the yellow footprints painted on the concrete in front of us. Every recruit snapped to attention, our bodies trembling as we took our first steps into a world of relentless discipline and control.

After a brief round of instructions, more yelling, really, we were led to a changing area. Our civilian clothes were stripped away, and in exchange, we were issued military uniforms. I later found out that "issued" didn't mean "free." Most of our first two months of pay would be taken to cover the cost of those uniforms. Afterward, we were assigned a footlocker and a rack in the squad bay. This, we were told, would be our home for the next three months.

Three months; it felt like an eternity stretched before us, a grueling challenge that would test every fiber of our being. We quickly stowed our belongings, locked our footlockers, and training began in earnest.

The days in boot camp blurred together in a haze of early mornings and brutal routines. We woke up at the crack of dawn, 5:00 AM, though we could never be sure since no one was allowed to have a watch. Time became a strange, abstract concept, slipping away without us ever knowing where it went.

It was unsettling, losing track of something so simple, so ordinary. We took it for granted until it was stripped away from us. I found ways around this purposeful problem. After only a few days I was able to determine the time of day based off of the position of the shadows of the numerous palm trees that decorated the base. It wasn't long until the lack of our watches was meaningless when it came to telling the time of day.

Our days started with physical training; push-ups, sit-ups, pull-ups, ten-count body-builders, and endless other exercises that pushed our bodies to their limits. Then came the long runs, mile after mile, our feet pounding the ground in unison. The rhythm of our steps became as familiar as our own breath. After PT, we'd march to the chow hall, where we were given just a few minutes to wolf down our food. Five minutes, maybe less. Fortunately, I had always been a fast eater, but others weren't so lucky. It didn't take long for them to learn that in boot camp, speed was survival.

After breakfast, we showered, then spent hours in the classroom. There, we learned the essentials; command structure, general orders, combat skills, and everything else required of a Marine. It was mind-numbing at times, but we had no choice but to absorb it. The tests at the end of boot camp weren't easy, and no one wanted to be held back.

The attrition rate was staggering. We started with 120 recruits, and by the time graduation rolled around, only 82 remained. The numbers were sobering, especially since we gained several recruits from other platoons who had been dropped along the way.

Two months into the ordeal, we left the routine behind and headed to the rifle range. I had never fired a rifle before, and my first shot startled me. The sensation of holding a weapon that exploded with controlled power in my hands was unnatural and unnerving. Yet, over the next several days, we learned everything there was to know about the M-16. How to shoot it, disassemble it, clean it, and troubleshoot it. By the time qualification day came, I had fired hundreds of rounds, but I still didn't feel ready. My instincts proved correct.

There were three shooting badges a Marine could earn; Marksman, Sharpshooter, and Expert. Each shot earned between zero and five points based on accuracy, and to qualify, you needed a minimum of 190 points. I was nervous, and my nerves got the better of me. I barely scraped by with a 191, earning the Marksman badge by a hair. It wasn't a shining moment, but I was relieved I didn't have to repeat the training.

* * *

The next challenge was mess and maintenance week. Rumors circulated about the horrors of working in the chow hall, and I prayed I would be placed on the maintenance crew. Naturally, my luck ran out, and I found myself on the mess crew. The rumors were true.

We worked eighteen to twenty hours a day, seven days a week. The exhaustion was bone-deep.

After a few days of only three or four hours of sleep, I felt like a zombie. My mind and body were no longer in sync. It was one of the hardest weeks of my life, and by the end, I seriously contemplated running away. I imagined making a break for it, disappearing into the night. But I knew better. Running meant failure, and failure meant losing the chance to earn the title of Marine. I held on, barely.

On the last day of mess duty, they told us we might have to stay another week if the next platoon wasn't ready to take over. That was the moment I nearly snapped. But luck, for once, was on my side. We were released from mess duty the following day, and I spent the next week trying to catch up on sleep.

Our final physical fitness test loomed ahead, and I had proven myself to be one of the most fit recruits in the platoon, possibly the entire battalion. My drill instructor pushed me hard, determined that I would earn the most physically fit Marine award, and I didn't want to disappoint.

The day of the test arrived, and the battalion gathered for the three-mile run. It was chaos at the start, 600 recruits jostling for space. I hung back, pacing myself. My drill instructor barked at me to pick up the pace, but I knew better. The others were running too fast. Sure enough, as we reached the halfway point, I passed them all one by one. By the time I reached the front, I was a full 200 meters ahead of the nearest recruit.

A drill instructor from another platoon ran beside me, impressed by my lead. He offered me advice, telling me I would burn out if I kept up the pace. I smiled, surged ahead, and left him behind. I crossed the finish line in 16:25, my personal best. The next recruit finished a full minute later.

I had done it. I had earned the title of most physically fit Marine, a huge moment of pride in my life. At graduation, my grandparents and parents were there to see me receive the award. I stood before the battalion, beaming as I was recognized, and I couldn't have been prouder when the battalion commander called us Marines for the first time. It was a moment I would never forget.

Chapter 41

After boot camp, going home felt surreal. I had never been away for more than a few days, and now, after three months, everything was different. My room, the space I had always claimed as my own, had been taken over by Ted. Most of my things were packed up into boxes and stowed away in the basement. I felt a strange sense of disconnection as I sifted through those boxes, searching for anything I might need for Marine Combat Training (MCT), my next step. A few small, familiar items found their way into my duffle, but I didn't linger in the past too long. There wasn't time.

My dad, however, seemed preoccupied with one thing; my weight.

"Still 135," I told him.

His disappointment was palpable. He had gained twenty pounds during Air Force boot camp, and apparently, he expected something similar from me. I understood why I hadn't gained a pound, though. They hadn't fed me enough. Most nights, I went to bed with a gnawing hunger, my stomach aching in protest.

Before long, I was back on a plane heading to California for combat training. MCT was a different beast, but in some ways, it felt easier. We were Marines now, already having earned the title. That seemed to afford us a little more respect. There was less screaming, more instruction. We learned how to assemble, disassemble, clean, and fire a variety of weapons. MCT wasn't just about the M16 anymore; we handled machine guns, grenade launchers, and even anti-tank rockets.

I had a leg up from the start thanks to my six-year contract, which came with an automatic promotion to Private First Class. It wasn't much, but it put me one rank higher than most of the other recruits, which led to my appointment as a fire team leader. It was a small responsibility, but a crucial one. I now had a team to look after.

One day, we ran a live-fire exercise. Real ammo loaded into our rifles meant we were constantly reminded of the danger.

"Keep your weapons pointed downrange," the instructors warned over and over again.

The last thing any of us wanted was an accidental shooting. As we charged down the course, shouting war cries, I kept a close eye on my team. That's when I noticed one of the Marines, he was on the far right, running full speed with his rifle pointed directly at the rest of us.

Instinct took over. I whistled and shouted at him, trying to get his attention, but the adrenaline and noise drowned out my voice. My heart raced as I flagged the instructor down. He saw the danger immediately, rushing in to yank the Marine off the course before anything catastrophic could happen. We'd all been inches away from disaster. It was a sobering reminder of how easily things could go wrong.

At night, we slept with our rifles. It wasn't just policy, it was survival. We had been warned that other units might try to steal our weapons while we slept. It was part of our training, teaching us never to let our guard down. Exhaustion made us vulnerable, and more than a few rifles disappeared from sleeping Marines. But I wasn't about to let that happen to me.

I devised a plan. The Marine sleeping next to me and I connected the straps of our rifles, crisscrossing them under our sleeping bags. This way, if someone tried to take either rifle, they'd have to drag one of us along with them. It was a simple but effective method, and I slept easier knowing my weapon was safe.

One night, chaos erupted. Our guide, the senior Marine trainee in charge, shouted at the top of his lungs. "Someone's trying to steal the guide-on!"

The guide-on was our platoon's flag, a symbol of pride and honor. Losing it would have been a humiliation. I jolted awake to the sight of our guide wrestling with a shadowy figure over the guide-on. The dark-clad intruder was strong and fast, but our guide held his ground. The rest of us, still groggy and disoriented, joined the chase as the mysterious man bolted into the night. We didn't catch him, but he didn't get the guide-on either.

Later, we found out the would-be thief was a Navy SEAL in training. Stealing a guide-on was a badge of honor for them, a daring challenge they often succeeded in. That night, though, we were lucky. We kept our flag and our pride.

MCT was relentless, but it taught us lessons we'd carry for the rest of our lives. Leadership, vigilance, and the constant awareness that danger could come from anywhere. We were Marines now, and the world was watching.

Chapter 42

At the end of Marine Combat Training (MCT), we were finally told what our next steps would be; our military occupational specialties, or MOS training. Most of the guys had jobs the instructors had heard of, roles that came with clear descriptions. But mine was different; MOS 5954. No one, not even the instructors, seemed to know what it was. All they could tell me was where I'd be going next; Memphis, Tennessee. That's where my technical training would begin.

* * *

After a long flight, I arrived in Memphis, and as soon as I stepped into the training facility, a Marine clerk at the front desk hit me with news that took me off guard.

After a quick look over my orders he said with a smirk, "Oh, you're MATCO. Marine Air Traffic Control and Operations. You're going to be here a long time," he stated with a chuckle.

His laughter sent a wave of unease through me. I wasn't sure what he found so funny, but I had a feeling I was about to find out. Memphis, it turned out, was a training facility where we were treated as little more than recruits. Full-fledged Marines had much more freedom once they reached the fleet; driving to work, weekends off, things that seemed like dreams to us. But here, in training, we were under a different regime.

Weekends? Forget it. While Marines in the fleet typically had duty once a month, we were on duty a quarter of the time, meaning one out of four weekends, sometimes more, were spent on base. And during the week, there were no regular eight-hour days followed by free time. We were locked into training for as long as they saw fit. The only real break came once you got through all your classes. For most guys, that meant attending "A" school for three to twelve weeks. Me? I was in for the long haul. MATCO wasn't just an "A" school, it was an "A," "B," and "C" school. One and a half years of training. It was the longest school on base, second only to one other in the entire Marine Corps.

When I got to the barracks, I was assigned a room and a rack. The space was small, impersonal, but functional. I threw my belongings in my new locker and sat on the bed, trying to absorb everything. It was the weekend, but I wouldn't start class for another month. A whole month of sitting around waiting for other Marines to arrive and fill out the class. In the meantime, I was assigned to a maintenance crew, which basically meant picking up trash around the base, and another full month added on to my already lengthy stay.

The barracks were divided into floors, or "decks," and duty rotated from one deck to the next each week. My deck, on the second floor, was on duty the moment I arrived. That meant fire watch at all times except during school hours, and being restricted to the base. We couldn't leave except for chow, physical training, or class. If your deck wasn't on duty, you had more freedom after school, though you still had a curfew and had to be back for morning muster at

6:00 AM. On weekends, if you were off duty, you could leave for the whole weekend as long as you were back by Monday morning.

Duty wasn't just about fire watch, though. It also meant a rotation of shifts, and the one shift every Marine hated was the midnight to 2:00 AM watch, known as "balls to two." Midnight, in military time, is represented by a set of zeroes, which, to some Marines, looked like a set of "balls." The shift lived up to its name, it was miserable, breaking up your sleep in the worst way possible.

Two weeks in, I got my first real taste of life in the barracks. It was the middle of the night when my drunk roommate and his equally drunk friends burst into the room. Before I knew it, they grabbed me, dragging me out of bed. Laughing and shouting, they hauled me into the showers and turned on the freezing cold water, tossing me under the spray.

"Look at your newb, he looks like he's gonna cry!" they taunted, their voices echoing in the tile-lined room.

I lay there, drenched and shivering, my body numb from the cold. Part of me wanted to lash out, to use every combat skill I'd learned at boot camp to knock them on their asses. But it was four against one, and they knew the same moves I did. It wasn't worth it. I dried off as best I could and crawled back into my rack, seething.

The next day, I went to the deck NCO, the senior Marine trainee in charge, to report what had happened.

"My roommate tossed me into the shower last night around two," I complained, expecting some kind of action.

The NCO smirked. "Oh, he shower-mustered you, did he?"

Behind him, the deck scribe, the guy in charge of assigning the duty roster, grinned as well. I quickly realized I wasn't going to get much sympathy.

"Looks like it," I replied, keeping my voice steady.

"You're not going to be trouble for us, are you?" the NCO asked, eyeing my name tape.

"I don't want trouble. I just don't want to be thrown in a cold shower in the middle of the night," I said, trying to keep things calm.

"You don't like being woken up in the middle of the night, huh?" the scribe chimed in, his grin widening.

"Do you?" I shot back.

The scribe exchanged a glance with the NCO. "I think this guy needs the balls to two watch, don't you?"

"I think he just might," the NCO agreed, his smirk deepening.

I didn't know what that meant at the time, but I was about to find out. From then on, every time I had duty, I was assigned the balls to two watch. The worst part of the schedule was how it ruined your sleep. I couldn't escape it. In hindsight, I should've kept my mouth shut, complaining had only made things worse.

Chapter 43

I had always been careful with my money. I didn't spend much on entertainment, so I managed to save a good chunk of what I earned. One afternoon, while walking past a car lot, I made a spontaneous decision; I was going to buy myself a car. Sure, I couldn't drive it to school, but I'd have it for the weekends when I had time off.

After browsing through the options, I found the perfect car; a blue Ford Festiva. It was economical in every way, and it reminded me of home. My dad had owned the exact same model, down to the color. The familiarity was comforting, and after purchasing it I spent my afternoons working on the car, making sure it ran smoothly. Before long, I had it purring like a well-oiled machine.

A few weeks after I got my car, some Marines in class started talking about a dance club in town. It was a popular spot they were planning to hit up that Friday night, and they invited me to come along. I couldn't dance, but the invitation felt like a big deal. I hadn't really been out before, at least not like this; I decided to go.

The excitement hit me immediately. I wasn't sure how to behave, what to wear, or what to expect. So, I put on what I considered my best outfit and drove to meet the Marines at the address they'd given me. When I arrived, they greeted me with raised eyebrows.

"What are you wearing?" one of the PFCs asked, looking me up and down.

Confused, I glanced down at my clothes. "What do you mean?"

"Man, don't you have anything nicer?"

"This is my nicest outfit," I replied, a bit defensive.

The PFC chuckled. "Oh man. We've got to take you shopping. That outfit won't get you any women."

I shrugged off his comment. It seemed ridiculous to think women wouldn't be interested just because of what I was wearing. Shouldn't they want to get to know the real me? That's how it should work, right? I was undeterred as I followed them into the club. My heart raced. Maybe tonight I'd meet someone, finally. I'd never even kissed a girl before, let alone been on a date. But I was determined to try.

The club was a country dance hall, rustic and loud. The music was almost deafening. I'd never been to a school dance in high school, so I had no idea what to do. After a few minutes of the blaring music, I had to slip into the bathroom to stuff tissue into my ears, making sure it wasn't visible so I wouldn't embarrass myself.

I sat by the dance floor, watching in awe as people performed intricate dances in perfect unison. Each dance was different, some were for couples, others for individuals. The synchronized steps reminded me of military drills, which made me feel more comfortable. I started to pay close attention, watching as the dancers moved in repeating patterns. The same dances cycled through every forty minutes or so, giving me plenty of time to study them.

After a couple of hours, I thought I'd learned enough. With a mix of nerves and determination, I stepped onto the floor and tried my hand at one of the singles dances. I was terrible. My steps were completely out of sync, and I bumped into people more than once, but I didn't care. I was giving it my all. Slowly, I started getting the hang of it. By the end of the night, I had one dance almost down.

My confidence grew, and I thought, why not try a couples dance? I spotted a pretty woman and decided to go for it.

"Want to dance?" I asked, trying to sound casual.

She gave me a once-over before politely declining. "Uh, no thanks."

I wasn't prepared for rejection. My heart sank, but I swallowed the disappointment and tried again with another girl. The answer was the same; no. It hurt even more when I saw one of the women who had rejected me dancing with another guy moments later. He didn't seem like her boyfriend, just someone she preferred over me.

Throughout the night, I kept asking, but no one said yes. The rejections piled up, and I started to feel defeated. By the end of the night, I gave up on the couples dances and decided to focus on mastering the singles.

Every free weekend after that, I returned to the club. Within a couple of weeks, I had all the singles dances down. A few months later, I was even adding my own flair to the moves, impressing some of the regulars. Much to my surprise, a girl finally asked me to dance, which felt like a small victory. Still, when I asked her for her numbers afterward, she wasn't interested. She just wanted to dance, nothing more.

One night, after watching me strike out again and again, a Marine buddy of mine pulled me aside.

"I'm taking you shopping tomorrow," he said with a grin. "You need better clothes. I think it will improve your chances."

I was frustrated, but I agreed. Maybe he was right. Maybe a new wardrobe would change my luck. The next day, we hit the mall, and he helped me pick out some clothes that he swore would make a difference. I wasn't thrilled about spending the money, but I was willing to give it a shot.

The following weekend, I returned to the club, decked out in my new outfit. To my surprise, things started to change. Right away a girl asked me to dance, and for the first time, she seemed genuinely interested in more than just the dancing. I was too nervous to ask her for her number, still haunted by all the rejections.

But then, another girl asked me to dance, and later that night, a girl named Linda actually gave me her number. It was a small victory, but it felt monumental. Linda wasn't exactly my type, she had bleach-blonde hair and thick glasses, but I didn't care. After so many rejections, I figured this might be my only shot at having a girlfriend.

We went on a couple of dates, and things progressed faster than I had expected. After a few months, Linda asked me to be her boyfriend. Not long after, she told me she was getting kicked out of her parents' house. She had nowhere to go, and I couldn't bear the thought of her being homeless. So, I rented an apartment for her.

Even though I couldn't live off-base and had to stay in the barracks, I wanted to help her. Despite our relationship, I stuck to my Christian upbringing. I wasn't ready to have sex before marriage, and I wasn't about to compromise on that. But I was trying to be a good person, someone she could rely on, even though deep down, I wasn't sure if she was what I wanted. More than anything I just needed to feel desired and needed. Linda was the only one doing this for me.

Chapter 44

A month after Linda moved into the apartment, she made it clear that she wanted to get married. At first, I hesitated. It felt too soon, too rushed. But soon enough, my deeper fears got the better of me. I didn't want to lose what I thought was my only chance at love. The truth was, I wasn't even sure I loved her. I convinced myself that love would come in time, that it would grow naturally as our relationship progressed. Linda, on the other hand, was dropping hints left and right, and eventually, I caved. I bought a ring and proposed. She accepted it with a bright smile and put it on her finger without a moment of hesitation.

Not long after that, Linda's car broke down. She told me she needed a new one, so we started car shopping. I was only a lance corporal at the time, and my paycheck barely covered my own expenses, let alone the cost of a second car. We looked at several, but none of the options seemed to satisfy her. Linda had her heart set on something flashier, something I couldn't afford. Then we came across a dark green Pontiac Firebird. Her eyes lit up when she saw it.

"This is not a car we need right now," I said, trying to be practical.

"But it's so pretty," she cooed, batting her eyes and rubbing my arm.

I tried again to reason with her. "We should get something more reasonable. We can't afford this."

She pouted, her lips trembling. "But I love this one."

And just like that, I gave in. "Okay, if you love it, then I'll get it for you."

I wanted her to be happy. She was going to be my wife, after all, and I was determined to make her feel special. So, I bought the car, even though I knew deep down it wasn't the right decision.

* * *

Word of my engagement spread quickly among my fellow Marines. A few weeks later, one of my classmates approached me with a serious expression on his face.

"You're not going to believe this," he said, lowering his voice. "I saw your fiancée going into the barracks with another Marine."

I froze. "Are you sure it was Linda?"

He nodded, looking me in the eye. "Oh, I'm sure. I know what I saw."

I didn't want to believe him. I couldn't. "That can't be right. You must be mistaken."

"I'm not mistaken. It was her, one hundred percent," he insisted, unwavering in his certainty.

Despite his confidence, I refused to let doubt settle in. Linda wouldn't do that to me, she loved me. That night, I asked her about it, but she brushed it off, saying she had been out job hunting and had no time for anything else. She sounded so convincing, and I believed her. Why wouldn't I? She was my fiancée, the woman I trusted.

* * *

One weekend, Linda and I decided to head down to the club on base. I got her onto the base with my ID and into the club without any issues. Not long after we arrived, Linda's face lit up when one of her friends approached with news that clearly thrilled her. At first, I had no idea what was going on, but I was about to find out. As we made our way into the club's lobby, Linda mentioned that a few pilots were there that evening. She pulled me aside and asked me for a favor I wasn't expecting: she wanted me to wait in the lobby and not go inside. She said she needed to talk to the pilots alone.

I was furious, and to this day, I can't understand why I agreed. I sank into one of the lobby chairs, watching as Linda and her friend disappeared into the club. Hours went by, and my mind was racing with thoughts about what might be happening inside. I wanted so badly to storm in, confront her, and end our engagement right then and there. I wanted to walk out and leave her with those unseen pilots; but I didn't. I was convinced that Linda was the only person who would ever love me, the only one who had ever shown me tenderness. I felt trapped, stuck in a psychological pit I couldn't seem to climb out of. So I stayed, waiting.

Eventually, Linda came back out, clearly pleased with herself. She walked over to me with a satisfied smile. I wanted to leave her right then, but I couldn't bring myself to move. I told her I wasn't happy about what had happened, but she brushed my feelings aside. She took my hand and led me out of the club, but in that moment, something inside me broke. The trust I had for her was shattered, and I knew our relationship would never be the same. I hoped it was just a one-time thing, but deep down, I feared otherwise. And she would prove me right.

* * *

A few weeks later, I told Linda that I wouldn't be able to see her that weekend because I had been assigned duty. Typically, I wouldn't be able to leave the base during duty, but sometimes exceptions were made. Halfway through the weekend, the deck NCO approached me with a friendly grin.

"Why don't you go see your woman?" he suggested.

I blinked, surprised. "What?"

He gave me a knowing smile. "I'm giving you permission to go see her. Just keep it quiet, don't let anyone catch you."

I couldn't believe my luck. "Thanks!"

He nodded, and I bolted out of there. I jumped into my Festiva and sped toward the apartment, eager to surprise Linda. My excitement grew as I pulled into the parking lot. I slipped the key into the door and turned it, but before I could push it open, I heard hurried footsteps on the other side. The door stopped halfway, blocked from the inside. Linda's face appeared in the crack, and she looked startled, and was breathing heavily. In her hand, she held a can of mace, pointing it straight at me.

"What are you doing here?" she asked, her voice shaky, eyes wide.

I frowned. "I'm here to see my fiancée. What's going on?"

"You're supposed to be on duty," she stammered.

"I am, but I got permission to leave. Are you going to let me in?"

She hesitated, then slowly opened the door. I stepped inside, and immediately, something felt off. The air was thick with tension, and Linda's demeanor was all wrong.

"Is someone here?" I asked, the suspicion rising in my chest.

She didn't answer.

I walked through the apartment, my heart pounding. When I reached the bedroom, my worst fear was confirmed. Another Marine was sitting on the edge of my bed, his face pale and full of dread. He didn't say a word. Neither did I. We stared at each other for a moment, the weight of the betrayal sinking in.

Finally, I broke the silence, my voice surprisingly calm. "Get out of my house."

The Marine hurried past me without a word, his head down. I returned to the living room where Linda stood, looking guilty and scared. I held out my hand.

"Give me the keys to the apartment and the Firebird," I said firmly.

She didn't argue. She reached into her pocket and handed me the keys. I stared at her, the anger and hurt swelling inside me. "And the ring."

She hesitated, but when she saw the resolve in my eyes, she slipped the ring off her finger and handed it to me without protest. The Marine had already left, and a moment later, Linda followed him out the door. They got into his car and drove away, leaving me standing in the silence of the apartment I had rented for her, the one I had foolishly thought would be our home.

I had trusted her completely. I never thought she would betray me like this. My confidence in love, in people, was shattered. I then wondered if I would ever trust a woman again.

Chapter 45

The breakup with Linda hit me hard. It felt like a crushing weight I couldn't shake off. When word spread through the ranks, my fellow Marines invited me to a house party. One of them was married and had a place off-base, a rare luxury in our world of barracks and shared spaces. I wasn't in the mood for a party, but the idea of distraction was tempting. I needed something to numb the pain, something to drown out the ache of betrayal.

When I arrived, the party was already in full swing. Music boomed from speakers, and laughter filled the air. People passed drinks back and forth, the clink of bottles adding to the lively atmosphere. As soon as I stepped through the door, the host greeted me with a wide grin.

"What would you like to drink?" he asked, holding up a pitcher.

I hesitated. "I don't know. Never drank before."

His eyebrows shot up in surprise, then his grin widened. "Well, we've got to fix that. Here, try this."

He poured a large glass from the pitcher, a bright red liquid that looked like Kool-Aid, and handed it to me. I wasn't sure what to expect, but I was curious. People always talked about alcohol easing pain, dulling emotions, making everything fade. I needed that more than ever.

"What's this?" I asked, peering at the drink.

"It's called a hurricane," he said, his grin still plastered on his face.

I didn't realize it then, but he was probably trying to get me drunk for his own amusement. I didn't care. I was too heartbroken to think about the consequences.

"Is it good?"

"Try it," he urged.

I took a sip, and to my surprise, it tasted sweet, like fruit punch. I couldn't even taste the alcohol, though I wasn't entirely sure what alcohol was supposed to taste like.

"It's good," I told him and started drinking it like it was Kool-Aid.

I finished the glass in a couple of minutes, still feeling nothing. Not even a buzz. So, I wandered back into the kitchen for another.

When the host saw me, his eyes widened. "What? You're done with that already?"

"Yeah," I said, holding up the empty glass. "Can I have another?"

He frowned. "That was almost thirty ounces, man."

"It must be weak," I shrugged. "I don't feel a thing."

Knowing just how strong he had made the drink his amusement quickly faded. "Okay, you need to sit down. You're cut off," he said, his expression serious now.

He probably realized I had no idea how to handle alcohol, and he was right; I didn't. Feeling a little disappointed, I walked to the couch to sit down. Maybe drinking wouldn't work after all. I looked around, trying to find another distraction, but as soon as I was about to sit back down, I noticed something strange. The corner of the room started to shake. I blinked and looked again, but the shaking only got worse. Then the entire room began to spin.

My head swam as I lost my balance. I attempted to sit down hoping to get there before I lost all control, but instead, I stumbled toward the floor. On the way down, I hit the edge of the coffee table catapulting several drinks into the air. Liquor and mixers splattered the walls, ceiling, and new carpet.

The host rushed over, his face a mask of frustration. "Get him out of here!" he shouted.

I had made a mess of his apartment, and I knew his wife was going to freak out. Two Marines grabbed me, one under each arm, and half-carried, half-dragged me to one of their cars. They drove me back to the barracks and handed me over to the Marine on duty.

"Make sure he gets to his rack, will you?" one of them said before they sped off, leaving me in the hands of the duty Marine.

The duty Marine wasn't amused. He gave me a glare before dragging me to my bunk. My roommate, fast asleep on the top rack, stirred at the noise but didn't seem too bothered.

As the duty left the room, he muttered to my roommate, "Make sure he doesn't leave."

My roommate groaned, half-awake. "Sure, sure." He turned over and went back to sleep, leaving me to my own devices.

As I lay there, the spinning room started to settle a bit, and I felt an odd curiosity. I had never been drunk before, and I wondered what it would be like to explore in this state. I should have left well enough alone and slept off my drunken state, but I wasn't smart enough for that. I wasn't content staying in bed, so I quietly got up and crept toward the door. My roommate, completely out of it, didn't notice. I made it down the hall and into the stairwell before the duty Marine spotted me.

"Where do you think you're going?" he barked, giving chase.

I tried to move faster, but my coordination was off, and I stumbled up the stairs. The Marine caught up with me, grabbed my arm, and dragged me back to my room, tossing me onto my bunk like a sack of potatoes.

"Stay in your rack, or I'll hold your roommate responsible," he warned, glaring at both of us.

My roommate groaned in protest, but the Marine was already out the door. The second he left, I was up again. There was no way I was staying put. I needed out. The spinning had stopped just enough for me to think more straight, or at least what I thought was straight. If I couldn't go through the door, there was always another way. My eyes landed on the window.

Without a second thought, I pushed it open. The frame creaked, and I began squeezing through the narrow opening. As I hoisted myself over the ledge, my roommate woke up again and saw me halfway out.

"Damn it, stop!" he shouted, but it was too late.

I was already outside, teetering on the edge of the second-story balcony. My roommate, still groggy, leapt off his bunk in a panic and tripped over the glass of the open window, shattering it. His hand was cut, blood spilling onto the floor, but I didn't notice. I was too focused on my escape. I jumped from the balcony, landing awkwardly on the ground below. I felt a sharp twist in my knee but ignored it. I was free, or at least I thought I was. I took off running across the base, my feet barely touching the ground. It was exhilarating, like I was floating.

That feeling didn't last long. The siren of an MP vehicle blared behind me, and a spotlight cut through the darkness, sweeping across the field. I ducked into the shadows, but it didn't take long for them to find me. For a moment, I thought about giving up. But then I heard the voices of the MPs closing in, and something inside me snapped. They weren't going to catch me; not tonight. I took off running again, dodging through alleyways and backstreets, the MPs in hot pursuit.

They tried to surround me, but I was too fast, slipping past them like a shadow. Each time they thought they had me, I'd dart away, laughing to myself. It was a game now, a twisted game of cat and mouse. But then, I heard it, a low, menacing growl. I glanced over my shoulder and saw the MPs bringing out their secret weapon; a K-9. The dog barked, straining at its leash, eager to chase me down. The game was over. I wasn't about to get torn apart by a dog or shot by an MP.

"GET DOWN ON THE GROUND!" one of the MPs yelled.

I complied, dropping to my knees and pressing my face into the dirt. Seconds later, I felt the hot breath of the dog on the back of my neck.

"You're lucky," the MP muttered as he cuffed me. "I was about to let my dog take you down."

I wanted to say, you're lucky you had that dog, or you never would've caught me, but I kept my mouth shut. They drove me back to the base, taking me straight to the Staff Duty Officer's office. When the cuffs came off, I stood in front of the SDO, bracing myself for the worst.

He looked at me with a mix of disappointment and disbelief. "Really?"

I shrugged. "What?"

"You've been leading the MPs on an hour-long chase," he said. There was a strange undertone in his voice. Part anger, part amusement.

I couldn't help but wonder if, beneath his frustration, he found it a little funny that I'd made the MPs chase me for so long. After all, Marines are part of the Navy, but there's always been a friendly rivalry between us. Maybe, in some small way, I'd won a point for the Corps that night. But whatever he felt, I knew one thing for sure; I was in big trouble.

The base was a pressure cooker, and the tension between the Navy and the Marines had been simmering for weeks. The sailors were tired of us taunting them on their own turf, and some of them weren't afraid to show it. More than a few Marines, caught alone at the wrong time, had been jumped and sent to the hospital by unruly sailors looking to settle the score. It was starting to feel like open season on anyone not moving in a pack.

Our combat training was worlds ahead of what the Navy guys received, and that kept us confident. If we stuck together in groups, we were safe. But the brass wasn't taking any chances. They made it mandatory for all of us to take extra hand-to-hand combat training and boxing lessons. I wasn't sure if it was the best approach, it felt like fueling a fire that was already burning, but it did give us a boost of confidence. At least we knew how to defend ourselves if it came down to it. And with the growing tension, it seemed like a matter of when, not if.

To put it plainly, there were harsh feelings on both sides. That's why, when the Staff Duty Officer stood in front of me, looking both pissed off and vaguely amused, I decided to play off that unspoken rivalry between us and the Navy.

"They're squids," I said, shrugging. "They couldn't keep up with a Marine if they tried."

The S.D.O. tried to maintain his stern expression, but I caught the flicker of amusement in his eyes. He shook his head and sighed, trying to suppress the laugh that was bubbling just under the surface.

"Alright, come with me, you knucklehead."

He led me back to the barracks, his heavy boots thudding against the concrete in time with my own quieter steps. Then the reality of trouble hit me hard.

"You're secured for the rest of the weekend," he said sternly. "Let's hope the Sergeant Major's in a good mood on Monday."

His words hit me like a punch to the gut. My heart sank into my stomach as I followed him inside. Not only had I lost my freedom for the rest of the weekend, but further unknown consequences hung in the balance. I had never even met the Sergeant Major, and now I was about to meet him under the worst possible circumstances. Not exactly the kind of first impression you want to make with your superiors.

The S.D.O. left me in my room, and just in time. As soon as he was gone, a wave of nausea rolled over me. I was pretty sure it was from the alcohol still churning in my stomach, not the anxiety gnawing at me over the impending meeting with the Sergeant Major. Either way, I bolted for the bathroom and spent the next hour praying to the porcelain god, emptying what felt like my entire body into the toilet.

I spent the rest of the night on the cold tile floor, my head resting against the wall, eyes half-closed in misery. Every so often, another wave of nausea would send me scrambling back to the toilet. By the time morning came, I was a wreck; sweaty, dehydrated, and still feeling like my head was on a slow spin cycle.

To make matters worse, I had to serve duty with the Marines from the third deck that day. Word had spread like wildfire about my drunken escapades the night before. The second I showed up, the jokes started flying.

"Well, look who it is! The second deck jumper!" one of them called out, and the rest of the guys broke out in laughter.

I cringed inwardly. Second deck jumper? The nickname stuck, and no matter how much time passed, it was a constant reminder of that one ridiculous night. That nickname followed me for the rest of my time on base, like a shadow I couldn't shake. I was lucky, though, in more ways than one. That night could have ended so much worse. If I'd landed wrong while jumping, if the MPs had escalated things during the chase, if my drunken stunt had caused serious harm to anyone other than myself. The mostly avoided disaster couldn't have been understated.

And as for the Sergeant Major? I was even luckier there. He didn't see my actions as worthy of his attention, and I avoided what could have easily been a much harsher punishment. I could've lost a stripe for that stupidity, but somehow, I managed to skate by. Apparently, the embarrassment of being known as the "second deck jumper" was enough punishment on its own. At least I survived to learn from it, and hopefully, grown a little wiser. But in the back of my mind, I knew I'd be hearing that nickname whispered behind my back for a long, long time.

Chapter 46

It was around that time in my life, while sitting in a classroom, that a fellow Marine reintroduced me to something I had not seen in over fifteen years; magic. Not the David Copperfield stage-show kind of magic, but something small, personal, almost intimate. He carried a deck of cards in his hand like it was an extension of his own body. Without saying much, he casually shuffled the cards and then turned to me.

"Pick a card," he said with a smirk, holding the deck out for me.

I humored him, choosing a card. I don't even remember what it was now. I returned it to the deck, and he went through the usual theatrics of mixing up the cards, his hands moving with practiced ease.

A few seconds later, he pulled out a card from the deck and held it up. "Is this your card?" he asked, confident.

I looked at the card. It wasn't even close. "No," I replied, feeling a twinge of disappointment. I figured he'd messed up the trick and that would be the end of it.

But he wasn't deterred. He smiled, set the card face down on the table, and drew another. "How about this one?"

Again, it wasn't my card. "No," I said, starting to lose interest. At this point, I was sure he'd blown it.

But he kept going, pulling out a third card, then a fourth, neither of which was mine. With the four cards now laid out in a neat row on the table, he leaned back and asked me to point to two of them. I did, feeling increasingly like this was a waste of time.

He picked up the two I pointed to. “Are either of these your card?”

They weren’t. “No.”

He asked me to point to another one, and again, it wasn’t my card. Now, there was only one card left, facedown on the table. By now, I was beyond skeptical.

“How much do you want to bet that this last card is yours?” he asked, eyes glinting with that same cocky smile.

“It’s not,” I said, certain of it.

“If you’re so sure, bet me,” he insisted, leaning in.

“I don’t have any money,” I said. As a lance corporal, I was pretty much perpetually broke.

“Okay,” he said, grinning wider. “How about twenty push-ups?”

I was positive the card wasn’t mine, so I shrugged. “Alright, sounds good.”

He flipped the last card over with a flourish, and there it was; my card. I couldn’t believe it. My jaw dropped as I stared at the card, trying to make sense of how he had pulled it off. It didn’t seem possible, and yet, it had happened right in front of me. After doing my twenty push-ups, I begged him to reveal the secret.

“How’d you do it?” I asked, desperate to know.

He smiled and shook his head. “A magician never reveals his secrets.”

I tried again the next day. And the day after that. I hounded him for days, determined to learn the secrete. He kept brushing me off, but my persistence eventually wore him down. Finally, one day, he caved.

"Fine," he said with a sigh, "I'll show you how it's done."

When he revealed the secret, I was floored. It was so simple, almost insultingly easy. I had been utterly convinced that it must have been some complex sleight of hand or intricate manipulation, but the truth was far more straightforward. I'd been fooled, completely, and I couldn't help but laugh at myself.

The trick wasn't just clever, it was brilliant in its simplicity. And the effect; incredible. I had to learn it. I spent the next few days practicing obsessively, running through the moves over and over until I had it down perfectly. The first time I performed it for someone else and saw their eyes widen in disbelief, I felt the same rush I had when I'd first seen it.

It wasn't long before I was performing the trick for everyone I could find. And to my amazement, people were just as impressed by my version as I had been by the original. I started to wonder if maybe I was onto something. Magic had grabbed hold of me in a way I hadn't anticipated. Of course, most of my time was still taken up with my duties, classes, and the usual demands of Marine life. I didn't dive into learning more magic at the time. But a seed had been planted. And though I didn't know it then, that little card trick had opened the door to something far bigger. It was the start of a journey I never saw coming, a passion that would grow into one of the greatest loves of my life.

Chapter 47

One weekend, a few of my Marine buddies and I decided to head to the PX, the military's version of a Walmart, where we bought everything we needed on base. Our barracks were the first of a row of six, all neatly lined up on either side of a walkway. As we walked, we noticed a group of Marines sitting outside one of the barracks at a picnic table, and one of them immediately caught my eye.

He was impossible to miss, standing at about six-foot-three and weighing around two hundred and forty pounds, this guy was massive. Even among Marines, where physical fitness was the norm, he stood out. Something about the way he looked at me, his eyes locked onto mine like a predator sizing up its prey, made me feel uneasy. I wasn't looking for trouble, but it seemed trouble had found me.

As we got closer, for no apparent reason, he stood up and blocked our path. His size alone was intimidating, and the way he grinned at me sent a chill down my spine. I didn't know this guy, and had never talked to him before, but it was clear he had singled me out for some kind of twisted amusement. Before I could even process what was happening, he lunged forward and grabbed me, wrapping his enormous arm around my neck and pulling me into a headlock.

I could feel the pressure instantly. My vertebrae popped as he tightened his grip, and I knew that if I didn't act fast, I'd be unconscious in a matter of seconds. I tried to push him off, but he was too strong. Panic surged through me, but then something kicked in, something primal. Without thinking, when he pushed into me I used his momentum and size against him, flipping his massive frame over my shoulder.

He hit the ground hard, but instead of being hurt or stunned, it only seemed to fuel his rage. I managed to hold him down like a wild bull full of fury. Now I was the one holding him in a headlock. The tables had suddenly turned and I was the one in control; for now.

"I'm going to kill you," he growled, his voice full of menace.

There was no doubt in my mind that he meant it. He was twice my size, and I knew I wouldn't survive if he regained control of the situation. My mind raced for a solution, and I realized I had only one option; run. I pressed down on his chest, using all my strength to push off him and spring to my feet. Without looking back, I bolted down the walkway as fast as my legs would carry me. I had a head start, and while he was stronger, I was faster. I didn't stop until I was sure he couldn't catch up with me.

I never saw that Marine again, before or after the incident. I still don't know why he picked me, or what he hoped to gain from attacking someone half his size. Maybe it was boredom. Maybe he just needed to feel like he was in control of something. Whatever the reason, I was just glad I'd managed to get away that day.

Chapter 48

Every weekend I had off, I was back on the dance floor. The music, the energy, the rhythm, it became my world. Sure, the ultimate goal was to meet women, but in the beginning, I was more focused on learning the dances themselves, perfecting my moves. I figured if I could get good enough, women would come to me, and I wouldn't have to deal with the one thing I absolutely couldn't stand; rejection.

It didn't take many attempts for me to learn how much I hated being turned down. Each rejection hit me like a punch, making me feel worthless. After a few tries, I decided I'd rather avoid the feeling altogether. If I didn't try, I couldn't be rejected, right? So, I stuck to my plan. I worked hard, mastering every step, every twirl, every beat of the music. And soon enough, it worked. I started attracting attention, though, as I eventually figured out, the wrong kind of attention.

One night, while I was lost in the music, I noticed her; a beautiful brunette. She was dancing nearby, her eyes glancing my way every so often, as if testing the waters. It was subtle, but unmistakable. She seemed interested. I hadn't planned on breaking my own rule, but something about her made me reconsider. Maybe it was the way she moved or how she kept dancing closer to me as the night went on. Besides, she was dropping me some distinct hints even I couldn't miss. Finally, I gathered my nerve and took the plunge.

"Would you like to dance?" I asked, half-expecting her to say no.

Her face lit up, and she smiled. “I was waiting for you to ask.”

That simple response sent a thrill through me. We danced for the rest of the night, laughing and talking between songs. Her name was Cindy, and she seemed genuinely interested in me. After hours of dancing, we ended the night with a kiss in the parking lot. It wasn’t my first kiss, but it was one of the few that made me feel something real. I was elated, floating on a cloud of disbelief. Someone actually liked me, someone I actually liked back.

I drove back to base in pure bliss, my mind replaying the night over and over. The next day, I couldn’t wait to call her. But this was before cell phones were everywhere. In the barracks, we had one payphone that the whole floor had to share. After waiting for what felt like forever, I finally got my turn. I dialed her number, nervous but excited. After a lengthy conversation we agreed to start dating. We went out a few times, and before long, I asked her to be my girlfriend; she said yes.

I still consider Cindy my first real girlfriend, someone who made me feel wanted, special, and I wanted back. She worked as an assistant manager at KB Toys, about a twenty-five-minute drive from my base. One weekend, I decided to surprise her while at work. I walked into the store, careful not to draw too much attention. She was busy, but when she saw me, she smiled and waved. I didn’t want to get her in trouble, so I kept my distance. She straightened some shelves nearby so we could talk a little while she worked.

After a while, I didn’t want to draw too much attention to our activities, so I decided to leave her to her job. She wouldn’t be off for another couple of hours, so I headed to the mall's arcade to kill some time. Nothing there really caught my interest, and my stomach started to rumble. I was craving McDonald's, and I knew there was one a few blocks away. It wasn't far, but I didn't feel like walking. So, I headed for my car in the parking lot.

That's when I heard a voice call from behind me. "Where you headed?"

I turned to see a tall man with dark greasy hair following me. Something about him felt off, but I couldn't place it. "McDonald's. Why?"

"That's perfect. I'm headed there too. Want a ride?"

I hesitated. I didn't like the idea, but at the same time, I had trouble saying no. I also hated being rude, and I especially hated rejecting people. After all, I knew what rejection felt like, and I didn't want to make someone else feel that way.

"Sure, I guess," I said, against my better judgment.

What harm could it do? I was a Marine, trained to handle myself, and it was just a quick trip to grab some food. We got into his car, and he drove us to McDonald's without incident. I thought that was the end of it. We got our food, sat down, and I figured he'd leave me alone after that.

But then, as we ate, he leaned in and asked, "Do you like gay porn?"

I froze. That had to be the strangest, most uncomfortable question anyone had ever asked me.

"No," I said, feeling a sudden need to get away.

He was quiet for a while, then asked, "Want to come back to my place?"

I stared at him, trying to keep my cool. "No," I said firmly.

He didn't seem phased and kept trying to make small talk, but I was done. As soon as I finished eating, I got up to leave. He followed me out, still persistent.

"Want a ride back to the mall?" he asked.

I looked at the long walk back and hesitated. I didn't want to be around this guy anymore, but I also wanted to get back to Cindy quickly. Against my better judgment, once again I agreed. That's when things went from bad to worse. Instead of driving back to the mall, he headed in the opposite direction.

"Where are you going?" I asked, my pulse quickening.

"We're going to my place," he said casually.

"I don't want to go to your place," I replied, my voice firm.

"I just need to pick something up."

I sat in tense silence as we pulled up to an apartment complex. He turned to me, unfazed. "Want to come up and watch some gay porn?"

"No!" I snapped. "Take me back to the mall, or I'll walk."

He must have sensed that I wasn't kidding, because without another word, he drove me back. I got out of the car and hurried inside, shaken but relieved. Looking back, I realize how lucky I was. I'd made a stupid, reckless decision, thinking nothing bad could ever happen to me. It was a hard lesson, but one I never forgot; never get into a stranger's car. Not everyone is as fortunate as I was.

Chapter 49

After several months of intense training, I finally graduated from my "C" school and was about to receive orders to join the fleet. It was a moment I had been working toward, but with it came a sense of dread. I knew what it meant for my relationships, especially with Cindy. Deployment was looming, and I couldn't ignore the impact it would have on us. One evening, I decided to break the news.

"I have some bad news," I said, my face heavy with the weight of what I was about to reveal.

Cindy looked up at me with concern in her eyes. "What is it?"

"I received my orders. I have to leave. I probably won't see you for four years."

Her expression dropped. "I knew this day would come," she said softly.

"Do you think we can survive being apart for that long?" I asked, hoping for reassurance but sensing her doubt.

Cindy sighed and met my gaze. "I don’t know. I hope so."

Her voice was thick with uncertainty, and I knew she wasn’t confident we could make it through such a long separation. I felt a pang in my chest.

"I wish I could take you with me," I said, the words coming out almost as a whisper.

"So do I," she replied.

The thought lingered in my mind, and before I realized it, I said, "I guess the only way I could take you with me is if we were married." I hadn't meant it as a real proposal, just a thought spoken aloud.

Cindy surprised me with her answer. "OK, let's do that."

I blinked, unsure if I'd heard her right. "Get married?" I asked, genuinely taken aback.

I knew we cared about each other, but I hadn't expected her to agree so quickly. I didn't think anyone would want to marry me.

"Yes," she said, smiling. "Why not?"

I paused, considering the idea. "Why not?" I repeated, a grin spreading across my face as the reality sank in.

* * *

A few days later, I bought a ring and got down on one knee to propose properly. Cindy accepted, and that night we spent the night together in my apartment. Until the point I met Cindy, I was still a virgin. My parents, devout Christians, had instilled in me the belief that sex should be saved for marriage. Now with our wedding plans set, I rationalized that it was close enough. The bonus to marring Cindy was I wouldn't go to hell for being with the woman I was about to marry.

As the weeks passed, we started planning our life together. We even picked out names for our future children; Joshua if it was a boy, Jackie if it was a girl. I took a month of leave to get married in my hometown, surrounded by my family. Cindy's family, however, didn't come. They were invited, but I think they boycotted the wedding, concerned about how quickly we were rushing into marriage.

We spent just one night together as husband and wife before I had to leave for my new duty station in Hawaii. I couldn't take Cindy with me right away because my orders were unaccompanied, meaning the government wouldn't cover her expenses, and I couldn't afford to pay for housing on my own with my small paycheck. My only hope was that my orders might be changed now that I was married, allowing us to live together.

Once I arrived in Hawaii, I went through the process of checking in with my new unit and settling into the singles barracks. As soon as I could, I went to the administration office to request a change in orders. To my immense relief, they modified my orders, and a couple of weeks later, I was granted a three-bedroom apartment on base. It felt like a dream. I immediately arranged for Cindy to fly out on the next available flight. When she arrived, it was as though everything in my life had finally fallen into place. I had a beautiful wife, a great home, and a promising future. For the first time in my life, I felt truly happy.

We quickly settled into our new life, making friends and attending parties with the other couples on base. But even with all this joy around me, I often found myself feeling awkward at these social gatherings. My social skills were still lacking, and I had little confidence. At parties, I often found myself sitting alone on the couch, watching others mingle, laugh, and have a good time, while I struggled to find a way to join in. I wanted to be part of the group, but I didn't know how to start a conversation or engage with people. I could tell some of them thought I was strange for being so quiet and reserved.

At one particular party, I found myself alone again, watching the fun from the sidelines. As I scanned the room, my eyes landed on a book sitting on the coffee table in front of me. It was an old book on magic that my friend had been reading. Curious, I picked it up and began flipping through the pages, intrigued by the secrets of magic it revealed. That's when I remembered the card trick I had learned back in Memphis.

"This is it!" I thought. "This is how I can break the ice at these parties!"

I asked my friend if I could borrow the book, and he agreed. From that point on, I spent my free time studying the book, practicing every trick and sleight of hand until I felt confident enough to try them out. At first, I doubted whether I could actually fool anyone. After all, I knew how the tricks were done, so they seemed too simple to work on people. But I needed an audience to test them on.

One evening, I knocked on my neighbor's door and offered to show them a few tricks. They welcomed me in, excited to see what I had learned. I performed a couple of illusions, hoping for the best.

"That's amazing!" they exclaimed, genuinely impressed.

I scrutinized their reactions, convinced they were just being polite. It was hard for me to believe that I had actually fooled them. But their enthusiasm encouraged me to keep practicing. I continued learning more magic from the book and honing my skills.

* * *

A few days later, while Cindy and I were walking through town, we stumbled upon a magic shop. I had never been inside one before and was fascinated by the array of tricks and illusions on display. I couldn't afford most of what they had, but when I asked the clerk for advice on getting started with magic, he smiled and handed me a large black book; Mark Wilson's Complete Course in Magic. I bought the book along with a couple of affordable tricks and took them home. With renewed excitement, I threw myself into learning more magic. Soon, I was ready to show off my skills at our next gathering.

* * *

A month later, at another party, I performed my tricks, and this time, a crowd gathered around me, captivated by my impromptu magic show. When I finished, people came up to me, impressed.

"How long have you been doing this?" someone asked.

"About a month," I replied honestly.

They were shocked. "What? Are you serious?"

I nodded, and they couldn't believe I was so new to the craft. As it turned out, I had a natural talent for magic, thanks to my hand-eye coordination. A few months later, I performed at another party, and afterward, a guest asked me a question that changed everything.

"How much do you charge for magic shows?"

It hadn't even occurred to me that I could make money from this. I didn't have an answer, but the idea intrigued me. Their son was having a birthday party the following week, and they wanted me to perform. I agreed, though I had no idea what to charge.

After the show, the parents asked, "So, how much do we owe you?"

Caught off guard, I blurted out, "How about twenty bucks?"

They happily agreed, though I later learned that most magicians at this time charged around $125 for similar performances. Still, it was a start. I still laugh at myself now at how ridiculously low I valued my skills back then.

Chapter 50

Marriage, in the beginning, felt like an absolute dream. For the most part, things were great between Cindy and me. We were building a life together, and I loved her more each day. But as the months wore on, the first cracks in our new reality started to show.

I worked every day, doing my best to provide for us, paying all the bills and covering every expense. Meanwhile, Cindy spent most of her time at home. I didn't mind that she wasn't working, but it became frustrating when she didn't seem to do much at all around the house. Every day, I'd come home from work to find the house in chaos, clothes scattered, dishes piled up, the floor littered with crumbs. Cindy, always on the couch watching TV, her eyes glued to the screen as if nothing else existed. The sight of it slowly gnawed at me.

One evening, after months of holding it in, I couldn't take it anymore. I tried to keep my tone as calm as possible, though frustration simmered beneath the surface.

"Would it be too much to ask for the house to be clean when I get home? Maybe have some dinner or something cooking?"

Cindy didn't even look up from the TV. "Sure, I can do that," she said, her tone dismissive.

I watched her for a moment, expecting some sign that she meant it. But when she didn't move, I sighed and started cleaning the house myself, just enough to make it bearable. I tried to keep my resentment in check. Maybe tomorrow would be better.

The next day, I came home hoping to see a difference. But nothing had changed. The house was still a mess, and there was no dinner cooking. It was as if my words the night before had meant nothing.

"Why didn't you clean the house today?" I asked, trying to keep my voice measured.

"Oh, I was going to get to it. I just haven't yet," Cindy replied, her eyes still fixed on the TV.

I bit back my frustration and headed into the kitchen to make dinner. Over the following weeks, things didn't improve. Every day, I came home to the same scene; Cindy on the couch, the house in disarray, and nothing to eat. The laundry had piled up so high it was spilling onto the floor, and I had reached my breaking point.

"If you're not going to help around the house, you need to get a job," I said one evening, my patience finally worn thin.

"OK," she said, her tone indifferent. She didn't seem fazed at all by my request, and that only fueled my frustration.

I waited, hoping to see some action, but nothing happened. Cindy made no effort to find a job, nor did she start helping around the house. More weeks passed with no change, and I decided it was time to take matters into my own hands.

I went down to the local Subway sandwich shop, one of the only sources of occupation on the base for civilians. I picked up an application, and brought it home. Handing it to Cindy, I said, "Fill this out."

She did, and I personally delivered it to the manager. A few days later, the manager called her in for an interview, and soon after, she was hired. Seeing her finally go to work gave me a sense of relief. At least now she was contributing.

Chapter 51

As a young adult, I reached a breaking point with the regular night terrors. I had endured years of these nightmares, relentless dreams where my father loomed, belt in hand, chasing me with the fury of all the punishments I'd suffered as a child. It was as if his presence haunted me even in sleep, and I could never escape the fear. I had become a Marine and fear was something I was trained to conquer, and one night, I decided I had enough. The torture had to end.

In the waking world, I was still terrified of my father. I became angry, an anger that had simmered for years, buried beneath layers of fear and helplessness. In my dream, the familiar scene unfolded; my father charging toward me, ready to punish. But this time, I didn't run. I wouldn't cower or hide. I stood my ground.

With all the pent-up rage I had carried for so long, I engaged him in a battle I had always been too afraid to face. It wasn't just a fight for control of the dream, it was a fight for my freedom. Every punch, every strike was fueled by years of suppressed emotion, by the scars his discipline had left on me, not just physically but mentally.

The battle didn't last long. In that dreamworld, I was stronger. I was ready to break free, and I did. I defeated him, not in the sense of revenge, but in reclaiming my power. The fear that had shackled me for so many years dissolved as I stood over him, victorious. In that moment, the nightmares finally ended.

But while I had conquered the phantoms of my sleep, I knew the real battles still lay ahead. The only nightmares left to face would be the ones waiting for me in the waking world, within the walls of my home, in the eyes of the father I still had to face some day. For now, I would have to endure until I could face him for real. But something had changed. In my dreams, I had won. Perhaps one day, I would win in reality too.

* * *

After a year of marriage, despite the minor bumps along the way, I found myself more in love with Cindy than ever. I wanted to take the next step and start a family. I slipped a note inside her birth control pill case, waiting for her to find it.

It read, "It's time!"

When she saw the note, she smiled, and we embraced, both excited to begin this new chapter. It didn't take long for her to get pregnant, though I admit, I had hoped we'd have a little more time to enjoy the process. A few weeks later, she told me the news; I was going to be a father.

The pregnancy went smoothly, and soon our daughter was born at Tripler Hospital in Hawaii. I was ecstatic. I had been looking forward to naming our child for months, and though we hadn't talked about it much lately, I remembered we had agreed on the name Jackie when we first got engaged. I couldn't wait to see if Cindy was still on board with that name or if she had new ideas. But when I brought Cindy and our newborn daughter home from the hospital, I was caught off guard. Cindy started calling her "Kim."

"Why are you calling her Kim?" I asked, confused. We had never discussed that name, not once.

"Because that's her name," Cindy replied, as if it were the most natural thing in the world.

"No, it's not," I said, growing frustrated. "We haven't decided on a name yet."

"I already decided," she said matter-of-factly. "Her name is Kim."

"Don't I get a say in naming my own daughter?" I asked, my voice rising.

"No," she said flatly.

"Why not?" I was becoming increasingly upset.

"Because I already filled out the paperwork at the hospital."

I stared at her in disbelief. She had filled out the paperwork behind my back, without even asking for my input. I felt betrayed, heartbroken. The woman I loved, the mother of my child, had made this monumental decision without me. I stood there, speechless, unable to process the enormity of what she had done.

The deed was done, and there was no easy way to change it. I didn't want to ruin the moment or cast a shadow over our daughter's homecoming, so I tried my best to let it go. But deep down, the hurt lingered. Cindy had taken away something important from me, the chance to be part of naming our child, to have a say in something so personal and significant. I tried to move past it, to focus on the joy of being a father. But even now, the memory still stings. That moment marked a shift in our relationship, one I couldn't ignore.

Chapter 52

Sports had always been a big part of my life, and that passion didn't fade when I joined the Marine Corps. I quickly got involved with my company's flag football team, and before long, I was one of their star players. At the time, I was married with a kid at home, and when they told me about practices being held after work, it seemed like they were optional. Most of the other guys were single and didn't have the same obligations I had. For me, getting away in the evenings was much harder. I was already in top physical condition, one of the most fit Marines in the company, so I figured they wouldn't mind if I missed the practices.

Game days, however, were a different story. I never missed a single game. I was always there, ready to play, so it came as a shock when I found myself sitting on the sidelines during most of our matchups. I couldn't understand it at first, why would they bench one of the fastest guys on the team when we needed to win? The frustration built as I watched from the sidelines, knowing I could help turn the game around.

It wasn't until after the season ended that I realized why they had kept me out of the game for so long. They were punishing me for not attending those "optional" practices. I'm sure, from their perspective, they were justified. Maybe they thought it was only fair to give playing time to those who had been there, sweating it out after work, every single day. In retrospect, I might have done the same thing if I were in their shoes.

But when they finally put me into the game, late in the season, it didn't take long for me to make my presence felt. On my third play, I intercepted a pass and ran it back for a touchdown. It was exactly what the team needed, we were losing badly, and that touchdown gave us a glimmer of hope. Despite the impact I made, I could feel that it didn't change their attitude. They still kept me sidelined for most of the plays, clearly trying to make a point.

I understood the lesson they were trying to teach. Sometimes, making a point can get in the way of winning, and in this case, it seemed like our team had put pride ahead of performance. Still, it was a valuable experience for me, one that taught me the importance of showing up, even when it feels optional.

* * *

I also joined the base wrestling team, eager to compete in a sport I'd always loved. But this was a different style than I was used to, freestyle wrestling, and it took a while for me to get the hang of it. Wrestling had always been a part of my identity, but freestyle was a different animal, and I had to adapt my strategies and techniques. After a few matches, though, I began to find my footing. I honed my skills and started to become one of the better wrestlers on the island by the end of the season.

When the state championship came around, I felt ready. I had a chip on my shoulder from high school when I had failed to make it to the finals. This was my chance to right that wrong, to prove to myself that I had what it took. I wasn't just determined to reach the finals; I planned to win. The matches were tough. Each one tested my endurance and mental fortitude, but I managed to defeat everyone on my side of the bracket. Each win brought me closer to that elusive title, and finally, I made it to the state finals. It was a huge moment for me.

Cindy, my wife, had come to watch the match, but on her way to the venue, she had a car accident. Thankfully, she wasn't seriously hurt, but my coach, finding out before the match, made sure she didn't tell me. He knew I needed to stay focused, and he didn't want me distracted.

When I stepped onto the mat for the final match, I came face-to-face with an opponent who exuded an air of confidence I hadn't seen before. This guy looked like he knew exactly what he was doing, but the Marine in me wasn't about to be intimidated. I believed I was ready for anything.

The first whistle blew, and within seconds, my world was flipped upside down; literally. This guy tossed me around the mat like I was a rag doll. I fought hard, but it was like wrestling a ghost, no matter what I did, he was always two steps ahead. I had never encountered someone with such skill and power.

What I didn't know going into the match was that I was up against a national champion. My coach hadn't told me, probably hoping to spare me any pre-match jitters, but it wouldn't have mattered. This wrestler was in a league of his own. For the first time in my wrestling career, I was tech-falled, utterly dominated. A tech-fall is when you get beaten by fifteen or more points, a major decision. The match was over quickly, sparing me from prolonged embarrassment, but the defeat stung deeply. My dream of winning a state championship had evaporated in the blink of an eye.

It was a hard pill to swallow, especially after coming so close, but that's how wrestling, and life, goes sometimes. Not every dream comes true. Now that I've retired from wrestling, I guess that dream of winning a state championship will remain just that; a dream. Some dreams are better left unfulfilled, I suppose. But the journey to the finals, the fight, and the lessons I learned along the way, that's something I can still be proud of.

Chapter 53

Around the time I was promoted to Corporal, I was sent back to the shooting range for the second time since boot camp. The last time I'd been there, I had earned a Sharpshooter badge, an improvement from my basic training performance, but I wasn't satisfied. My goal was to go beyond that. I wanted to earn the Expert badge, the highest honor on the range. I poured all my energy into refining my skills, studying precise shooting techniques, and making each shot count.

As the days passed, my confidence grew with every pull of the trigger. We spent five days on the range each year, and this time I was determined to make every one of those days count. By the time qualification day rolled around, I was nervous but focused, determined to keep my emotions in check. And at the end of that long, intense day, my hard work paid off, I earned my first Expert badge. It felt like a milestone, a sign that I was progressing, not just as a Marine but as someone who could set a goal and achieve it.

* * *

Not long after, I was assigned to a secondary mission. For the next six months, I was tasked with managing the barracks. It was a change of pace, far different from my usual electronics work. My responsibilities were simple but essential, I assigned rooms to Marines, kept track of the government-owned furniture in each room, and coordinated maintenance and repairs. It wasn't glamorous, but it was a nice break from the radio shop. Before long, though, I was back in the shop, fixing radios and diving into the technical work I was trained for.

* * *

Not long after, I was able to fulfill a long-standing dream for my grandmother and mother. When my mother was young, her father had left them for another woman, leaving my grandmother to raise four children on her own. She didn't have much education, so she took whatever jobs she could find, scraping by to keep food on the table. Life was hard, and they never had much money. But through it all, my grandmother had one dream she never let go of; she wanted to visit Hawaii. It seemed impossible back then, but now, with me stationed there and a spare room in my apartment, that dream was within reach.

My mom worked hard, saving every penny she could until she had enough to buy two tickets; one for herself and one for my grandmother. My sister, hearing about the trip, decided she wanted to come too, so she bought a ticket as well. None of them had ever been to Hawaii, and the excitement was palpable. I couldn't wait to have my family visit me, to show them the place I now called home.

At first, Cindy didn't seem to mind. She was fine with my family coming to stay for a couple of weeks. But after only a few days, something shifted. One night, I heard my mom and grandmother crying in their room. When I asked what was wrong, they told me Cindy had told them they weren't welcome anymore and that they needed to leave.

I was stunned; angry. I couldn't believe she would say something so cruel, especially knowing how much this trip meant to them. This was their dream vacation, a once-in-a-lifetime experience. I confronted Cindy, but it was clear she didn't care. She was ready for them to go.

Determined not to let her ruin their trip, I did everything I could to make my family feel welcome. I took them to Hanauma Bay, where we snorkeled with the vibrant tropical fish, and then we visited the vast pineapple fields before heading up to the North Shore, where the waves were enormous, surfers riding them with ease. It turned out to be a wonderful day, one of those perfect Hawaiian experiences. Despite the tension with Cindy, I managed to convince my family to stay for the full two weeks. I loved having them there, it felt too short, but I cherished every moment.

Cindy, on the other hand, couldn't wait to see them go. To this day, I don't know what her problem was with my family. They're some of the nicest people I know, and I never understood her hostility.

Throughout all of this, I kept trying to find ways to lighten the mood. I've always been a bit of a practical joker, something I got from my dad. Cindy, being the one I spent the most time with, often found herself on the receiving end of my pranks. To me, if a prank doesn't hurt anyone, it's harmless fun. But Cindy didn't share my sense of humor.

One day, while she was taking a nap, she left her glasses on the coffee table; I couldn't resist. Carefully, I removed all the screws from her glasses, placing them in a small jar for safekeeping. I didn't want to lose any of the pieces, the plan was to have a good laugh together, and then I'd put them back together.

Sure enough, when Cindy woke up, she went looking for her glasses. The moment she picked them up, the frames crumbled into her hands, just as I had planned. I burst out laughing, thinking it was hilarious. But Cindy didn't think so. She started screaming at me, her anger rising with each word. When she saw I wasn't taking her outburst seriously, she began to cry, gathering up the pieces of her disassembled glasses.

"I'll put them back together," I said, trying to suppress my laughter.

"Don't bother," she sobbed, storming out of the house.

To my surprise, she ran to the neighbors, telling them I had been abusive, taking apart her glasses and refusing to fix them. I couldn't believe it. She was already trying to paint me as some kind of monster, and I didn't understand why. After that incident, I could feel the tension from our neighbors, they seemed colder toward me, and I began to feel alienated in my own community. I didn't know where things had gone so wrong, but the weight of it all was starting to bear down on me.

Chapter 54

A few months after the tension between Cindy and me had reached a breaking point, my worst fears were realized. One afternoon, she told me she was going back home for a while.

"How long will you be gone?" I asked, trying to keep my voice steady.

She shrugged, avoiding my eyes. "I don't know."

A cold dread settled in my chest. "Do you want a divorce?"

Again, the same response. "I don't know."

A few days later, she packed her bags, took our daughter Kim, and flew back to Memphis. As I watched her leave, I couldn't shake the sinking feeling that she wasn't coming back.

My life, once built on the stability of routine, was suddenly in shambles. The emotional turmoil of losing my wife and daughter overwhelmed me. I was young and confused, lost in a sea of bad ideas, desperate for anything that could dull the pain. As I rummaged through my things, searching for some kind of comfort.

Much to my surprise, Cindy eventually came back. She stood in the doorway, her eyes tired but resolute.

"We need to work on our problems," she said. "Running away isn't going to fix anything."

I could hardly believe she was standing in front of me. I had been so sure she would never return, and yet, here she was, asking to rebuild what we had nearly lost. Relief washed over me, and I agreed to put in the effort to save our marriage. Slowly, we began to heal. We worked through our issues, talked more than we ever had before, and after a time, we found our way back to happiness.

* * *

A year later, I was promoted to Sergeant and put in charge of the shop. Cindy was invited to my promotion ceremony and pinned on my new chevrons. I now had four Marines working under me and was responsible for millions of dollars worth of government equipment. It was a massive responsibility for a twenty-four-year-old, especially since the systems we worked with were changing rapidly.

There were no set procedures in place yet, and we were essentially building the operations for the airfield from the ground up. It was chaotic, demanding, and stressful, but I thrived under the pressure. I repeated my performance on the shooting range that year, earning another Expert badge, and felt a sense of pride and accomplishment that had been missing for so long.

Life finally seemed to be back on track. I remember one particular afternoon vividly. Cindy and I were sitting in lawn chairs in the backyard, the sun warm on our faces. I had just finished mowing the grass, and Kim was playing in the yard, her laughter echoing through the air. We sat there, watching her, soaking in the peacefulness of the moment.

For the first time in a long while, I felt like I had everything I had ever wanted. A beautiful wife, a wonderful daughter, a home, a good job, and of all places, we were living in Hawaii. I couldn't have been happier.

In that moment, with Cindy by my side and Kim running carefree through the grass, life felt perfect. All the struggles, the fights, and the uncertainty seemed to fade into the background. We had made it through the worst, and now, we were stronger than ever.

Chapter 55

A year before my military contract was set to end, and just as I was beginning to think about life beyond the Marines, my world was turned upside down again. Orders came through; I was being deployed to Okinawa, Japan. The worst part wasn't just leaving, it was that it was an unaccompanied tour. I couldn't take my family with me.

The news hit me like a bombshell. But I had little time to dwell on the impending year apart. I had to make sure everything was ready for Cindy and Kim in my absence. We flew to Tennessee so I could arrange their living situation while I was gone. Cindy wanted to be near her family, so we agreed Memphis was the best place for her and our daughter. I secured an apartment, set it up with everything they'd need, and even bought Cindy a Nissan Sentra; something reliable to get her through the year without me.

I also made sure she had access to our life savings. I put over $20,000 into an account for her, a substantial amount back then, especially given how low military pay was. It had taken me more than three years to save that money, and I knew it would be enough to see them through, especially with rent in Memphis being just $300 a month. Cindy planned to go to school while I was away, and we reassured each other that we would reunite in a year. We believed we could make it through. At least, that's what we told ourselves.

When the day came to leave, the weight of the goodbye was heavier than I had anticipated. I bent down to kiss my two-year-old daughter, Kim, on the top of her head, lingering for a moment, trying to imprint her little face in my mind. I whispered a tearful goodbye, my hand resting gently on her head. I didn't know it at the time, but that would be the last day my daughter would ever live under my roof.

Leaving Cindy and Kim behind in Tennessee felt like tearing a piece of my soul away, but I had no choice. I boarded the plane and headed off to defend my country in Japan, where I'd spend the longest, hardest year of my life.

* * *

Life in Okinawa was brutal. I had never been away from my family for such an extended period, and the loneliness gnawed at me constantly. It felt like a deep hole in my chest that nothing could fill, an emptiness that consumed my thoughts, making even the most basic tasks difficult. It wasn't long until I fell into a deep depression, barely able to function some days. The stress took a physical toll, too. I started having dizzy spells and was eventually diagnosed with stress-induced vertigo.

To make things worse, I quickly realized that my presence in Okinawa wasn't even necessary. Our unit only needed one sergeant, and there were already two others. I felt like I had been sent there as a cruel joke. When I had spoken with the career planner before the assignment, I specifically asked not to be sent to Japan; anywhere but Japan.

He had looked me straight in the eye and said, "No problem. I'll see what I can do."

And yet, that's exactly where I ended up. To this day, I believe he did it to spite me. Maybe he was miserable with his own life and wanted to drag me down with him. Sometimes, I wonder if I would've stayed in Hawaii if I hadn't gone to him. If I'd just kept quiet, would I have spent the rest of my military career in paradise instead of being shipped off to the one place I didn't want to go? I'll never know. Japan cost me one dream but eventually gave me another.

The separation was hard on Cindy and Kim, too. Cindy and I talked on the phone almost every day, despite the cost. Hearing her voice was my lifeline. We wrote letters back and forth, and she sent me home videos that I cherished. One video, in particular, broke my heart. Cindy and Kim were sitting on the front porch, watching planes soar by at 30,000 feet. In the video, Cindy kept asking Kim the same question.

"Who's the bomb?"

"Daddy's the bomb!" Kim chirped back each time.

Watching that, my heart both soared and sank. I was missing my daughter's life. I should've been there, watching her grow, picking her up when she fell. Instead, I was thousands of miles away, trying to fill the void with fleeting phone calls and grainy videos. The heartache was almost unbearable. I could sense the strain it was putting on Cindy, too. The long distance was taking its toll on all of us.

At first, despite the distance, Cindy and I remained strong. We clung to the love that had carried us through so much already. Our phone conversations were filled with promises of our reunion, of how we'd be together again. We reassured each other that this was just a phase, a temporary hardship that we'd overcome. And for a while, we believed it. We were determined to make it through. But as the days turned into months, new cracks began to form.

* * *

Six months into my tour in Japan, I received a letter that shattered my already fragile world. It was from Cindy, and it wasn't the kind of letter I ever expected to read. Her words cut deep, she was threatening to take her own life if I didn't return home immediately. It was like a punch to the gut, leaving me reeling. The fear that I might lose her forever was suddenly very real.

I took the letter to my command, and they responded with what they thought was a solution. They gave me a choice; I could go back to Tennessee for a week to try and calm her down, but if I did, I would forfeit the chance to go home for Christmas. It wasn't much of a choice.

"If my wife kills herself," I told them, "there won't be any Christmas."

"Okay, if you're sure," they said.

I didn't hesitate. I was on the next plane out, heading home on emergency leave. When I arrived, I did everything I could to fix what had broken inside Cindy. It wasn't easy; there was a heaviness about her, a kind of sadness I had never seen before. But being in her arms again, holding Kim close every chance I got, it felt like I was filling up the emptiness that had been gnawing at me for months. For a brief moment, I felt whole again.

But the joy was short-lived. Just as quickly as I had arrived, it was time to leave again. The goodbye at the airport was brutal. As I stood at the gate, about to board the plane back to Japan, I looked into Cindy's eyes, and I saw something inside her break. It was as if a light had gone out, leaving only darkness behind. I tried to push the feeling away, but a cold dread settled in my chest. Still, I had to be strong. I put on a brave face and turned toward the plane, feeling as if I were walking away from something I couldn't fix.

Chapter 56

Back in Japan, I tried to hold everything together. I called Cindy every day, desperate to keep our connection alive. But I could feel her slipping away from me. She was growing distant, emotionally retreating into a place I couldn't reach from across an ocean. No matter what I said or did, the gap between us kept widening, and I was powerless to stop it. Each phone call felt more strained, and the impending doom I'd sensed at the airport grew stronger.

I didn't know it at the time, but Cindy had been confiding in my mom. They talked frequently, and my mom became aware of things I hadn't been told. Cindy had started going out to dance clubs at night, drinking and dancing with other men. When my mom voiced her concerns, Cindy brushed them off, claiming that I knew about it and was fine with it.

But she had never told me. I had no idea she was spending her nights in the company of other men, seeking comfort or distraction in ways I couldn't comprehend. The revelation, when it finally reached me, was like a slow-moving storm I could see coming but was powerless to stop. Everything was crumbling, and I couldn't do anything about it from thousands of miles away.

* * *

After that, Cindy's emotional distance only grew, I knew I had to find a way to occupy my mind. I needed something to distract me from the hollow feeling in my chest. Magic had always intrigued me, so I began practicing new tricks, throwing myself into it with the kind of focus that comes from desperation. I had always been shy, the kind of guy who kept to himself, but performing magic helped me step outside my shell. Before long, word had spread across the base, and I became known as the magician.

One day, Gunnery Sergeant McDaniel sought me out. He was a tough, no-nonsense Marine, and his presence made me uneasy. It wasn't common for a Gunny to track down a lower-ranked Sergeant like me unless something was wrong. As he approached, I braced myself.

"My name is Gunny McDaniel," he said, his voice authoritative. "I hear you perform magic."

I tried to act casual, but my nerves were on edge. "I do, a little."

"Would you mind coming to my barracks room after work today to show me a few tricks?" he asked, his tone firm but curious.

Now, I wasn't sure what to think. Why did he want me in his room? Was this some kind of setup? But Marines had a code, a bond of trust, and I decided to give him the benefit of the doubt.

"Sure," I said reluctantly.

He handed me a note with his barracks number and room details, and we agreed on a time. That evening, after a quick stop at my own room to grab my props, I knocked on his door, hoping he wasn't some weirdo. When he opened the door, he welcomed me in with genuine enthusiasm.

"So, you're a magician," Gunny McDaniel said, offering me a seat; his demeanor kinder and softer.

“Kinda. I know a few tricks."

He leaned forward, eyes gleaming with excitement. "Show me one."

I had been working on a trick I was particularly proud of, so I decided to perform it. Still in my military uniform, I waved my hand over the pen in my pocket, and slowly, the pen lifted itself out and floated into my hand. I handed it to McDaniel, waiting for his reaction. He stared at the pen, turning it over in his hands, clearly stumped. I figured he would laugh and call me out. After all, he was a professional magician, and I was just an amateur.

"How did you do that?" he finally asked, still baffled.

I couldn’t believe I’d managed to fool him. I was so new to magic, and the idea of keeping secrets wasn’t something I had embraced yet. So, feeling proud, I explained the gimmick and showed him how it worked.

He was impressed. "I've never seen that trick before."

"I invented it," I said, my chest swelling a little with pride.

"That's fantastic! Mind if I use it?"

"Go ahead," I replied, thrilled he thought it was good enough to use.

McDaniel seemed pleased and went to his locker, pulling out a large case. When he opened it, I was blown away by what I saw inside. It was filled with all kinds of professional magic props, the likes of which I had never seen before.

"Wow," I said, awestruck. "Where did you get all of this?"

"Magic shops," he replied, grinning.

He walked me through each item, explaining how the props worked and demonstrating their use. It was like stepping into a whole new world of magic, and I soaked up every bit of knowledge he offered. Before I left, he even gave me a few of his extra props as gifts.

"I'm also a hypnotist," he said, almost as an afterthought.

"That's cool!" I replied, though the idea made me uneasy.

My parents had always warned me about hypnosis, claiming it was evil and could lead to dangerous things. I'd been raised to avoid it like the plague.

"Have you ever seen a hypnosis show?"

"No," I admitted, unsure where this conversation was heading.

"Would you like to learn?"

I hesitated, my parents' warnings echoing in my head. "No thanks," I said, nervous.

McDaniel seemed surprised. "Why not?"

"My parents said it's evil," I told him, feeling a bit silly for saying it out loud.

He thought about it for a moment. "Tell you what. I have a show next week. Come as my guest, no ticket needed. If you don't like it, I'll never ask you again."

I considered it. Just watching wouldn't hurt, right? I wasn't going to be hypnotized myself, and I didn't have to perform it.

"Okay, I'll go."

Chapter 57

The following week, I arrived at McDaniel's show early and watched him set up the stage. When the show started, I was blown away. It was unlike anything I had ever seen before. People were laughing, participating, and reacting to his every command. It was mesmerizing. By the end of the show, I was hooked.

"I want to do that!" I thought, filled with a new sense of purpose.

McDaniel was pleased when I told him. The next day, he invited me back to his room and handed me a stack of books and videos. The pile was huge, almost too much for me to carry.

"Study all of this, then come back," he said.

I took the material back to my room and dove into it immediately. Every spare moment I had, I spent reading and watching the videos. It was a professional course in stage hypnosis, and I was determined to learn everything. I took notes, watched the important parts twice, and soaked in every bit of knowledge I could. It was the first time in months that I felt like I had a real purpose again.

* * *

A few weeks after my deep dive into learning hypnosis, a typhoon hit Okinawa, leaving us all stuck in the barracks. With nothing to do and boredom setting in, one of my fellow Marines got an idea. He knew I was a magician and also knew I was studying hypnosis.

"Why don't you try to hypnotize some of us?" he suggested, half-joking, half-hoping it would lead to some entertainment. My colleagues were well aware by now what I'd been spending my time doing.

To my surprise, the Marines were all for it. We gathered everyone interested into one of the larger rooms, and I did my best to set it up like Gunny McDaniel had done for his shows. I wasn't sure if it would actually work, I had never hypnotized anyone before, and I was nervous. But there was no turning back now. I began my induction, following everything I had learned and practiced from the books and videos McDaniel had given me. I could feel my heart racing as I went through the steps, praying it would work.

When I gave them their first suggestion, something remarkable happened, their eyes glazed over, and they followed my commands; it worked! I had actually hypnotized them. The Marines watching were stunned, and honestly, so was I. This wasn't supposed to be this easy, was it? Yet there they were, following my every suggestion like they were under a spell.

From there, the audience threw out suggestions, and we put on an impromptu show. It was hilarious, and everyone had a blast. I couldn't believe it, I had pulled off my first hypnosis show, and it was a success.

Chapter 58

Life in Okinawa was a world apart from my time in Hawaii. Hawaii had been a relatively comfortable, nine-to-five job with no deployments, but Okinawa was unpredictable. Deployments were regular and intense, something I had never experienced before. Each deployment lasted anywhere from thirty to forty-five days, and during that time, everything seemed to blend into one relentless cycle of work, exhaustion, and survival. The hours were non-stop, with little time to rest or recharge.

Showers were a rare luxury, and we subsisted on old MREs, meals ready to eat, that were likely leftovers from the Vietnam War. I'd never seen stale M&Ms before. Half the food was barely edible, and the rest? Well, if you wanted to avoid a bowel movement for two weeks, this food would surely help you make that dream a reality.

It was December, and the bitter cold was brutal beyond measure. Bone-chilling winds and freezing drizzle haunted us day and night. We spent most of our time outdoors, sleeping in old canvas tents that trapped no heat. At night, we wore as many layers as we could just to stave off the biting cold.

I still remember sitting through the night in a foxhole, drenched in freezing rain, my body numb. By the time my shift ended, I could hardly feel my limbs. I threw on every dry piece of clothing I had and crawled into my sleeping bag, hoping to warm up. It took nearly eight hours before I stopped shivering. Since that night, even the slightest breeze can chill me, and I never leave the house without a coat unless it's hot outside.

Entertainment was scarce on deployments. We had one CD, Matchbox Twenty, which, at the time, was one of my favorite bands. But after weeks of listening to the same songs on repeat, I couldn't stand to hear them anymore. It took nearly twenty years before I could listen to those songs again without wincing.

One night, close to the end of a deployment, several Marines approached me, looking for something to break up the monotony.

"You're a hypnotist, right?" one of them asked.

I'd performed maybe two or three shows by then, so I hesitated before answering. "Sure, I guess."

"Can you put on a show for us?"

I didn't know how I was going to pull it off in the middle of nowhere, with all the distractions around, no music, no script, just rain, wind, and a packed tent. Despite these huge obstacles, I agreed. The Marines setup the largest tent in camp, moved the racks to the sides, and gathered everyone not on duty. The tent filled quickly. I invited a few Marines to join me on the makeshift stage, and, despite my doubts, I managed to hypnotize them.

Without a plan, I started improvising, taking suggestions from the audience. One of those suggestions nearly cost me everything. I don't remember what the suggestion was, but suddenly one of the hypnotized Marines began looking for a weapon, ready to club me with a Kevlar helmet. I managed to snap him out of it just in time, but it could have ended very badly for me. I wrapped up the show quickly after that, grateful I hadn't been knocked out in front of everyone.

* * *

The next morning, as we packed up to leave, the camp was buzzing with talk about the previous night's show. Marines I didn't even know approached me, excited to chat about the performance. It was surreal, I went from being just another guy to a minor celebrity overnight. My confidence soared, but all I could think about was getting home. I hadn't spoken to Cindy in over a month, and I was desperate to hear from my family.

When we finally arrived back on base, my first shower was like heaven. I must have spent an hour washing off the dirt and grime that had caked onto my skin for weeks. It felt like I was purging my soul.

After that, I headed straight to my favorite restaurant and ordered a cheeseburger. That first bite, it was like tasting food for the first time. The flavors exploded in my mouth, reminding me how much I had taken for granted. The small luxuries in life that we barely notice become treasures when they're gone.

* * *

A few weeks later, Gunny McDaniel shipped back to the States. That left a void on the entertainment scene at the base clubs where he used to perform. I wasn't sure if I had the guts to step into his shoes, but I knew I wanted to. I went to one of the clubs and asked the manager if he'd let me perform in Gunny's absence.

I expected him to brush me off, maybe laugh at the idea of a rookie trying to fill McDaniel's spot. Instead, he agreed, saying he'd pay me with a steak dinner. It wasn't much, but it was something, and besides, I didn't care about money. I just wanted the experience.

Knowing I needed to look the part, I went into town and hired a tailor to make me my first professional performing vest, made with dark red Japanese silk. I bought a new shirt and pants to complete the look and practiced my show until I knew it inside out. Every part of the routine was committed to memory, and I rehearsed over and over again, making sure I was ready.

The night of the show arrived. I expected maybe twenty or thirty Marines to show up. After all, I was still a nobody. But when I stepped onto the stage, I was greeted by a packed club, over four hundred Marines and service members had shown up. The room was packed, standing room only, with Marines crammed into the aisles just to watch. I froze for a moment, overwhelmed by the size of the crowd.

If I failed, if I bombed in front of this crowd, my reputation would be ruined across the entire base. My heart pounded, and for a few agonizing seconds, my mind went blank. I couldn't remember my first line, my monologue, anything. Panic clawed at the edges of my thoughts. Then, suddenly, something clicked. The words I had rehearsed so many times came flooding back, and my brain switched to autopilot.

I launched into the routine, my nervousness melting away as I fell into the rhythm of the show. It felt almost surreal, like I was watching myself from a distance. Everything I had practiced flowed naturally.

I hypnotized twelve out of the fourteen volunteers, and before I knew it, I was deep into the show. The audience loved it, cheering and laughing with every suggestion I gave the hypnotized Marines.

When the show ended, I took my first bow in front of a roaring, standing ovation. The energy from the crowd surged through me, unlike anything I'd ever felt; it was electric. As I walked off the stage, my fellow Marines patted me on the back, congratulating me and praising the performance.

For the first time in my life, I felt truly accomplished. I had done something that people not only enjoyed but genuinely loved. It wasn't just about the applause or the pats on the back. It was the realization that I had found my passion, my calling. In that moment, I knew. I didn't just want to be a Marine anymore, I wanted to be a performer.

Chapter 59

As the months dragged on in Okinawa, things between Cindy and me only grew worse. At first, I blamed the distance, thinking that being halfway around the world was simply straining our relationship. The internet was new and still in its infancy back then, and I'd just gotten my first email account to stay in touch. I tried emailing Cindy, hoping it would help bridge the gap, but the coldness in her responses only mirrored the detachment I felt during our phone calls. Calling was expensive, but I still made it a point to hear her voice every other day. It didn't matter though, her voice, once so comforting, was now distant, indifferent. Sometimes even cruel.

I hoped it was just a phase, something that would pass if I just kept trying to bring her back to me. But it only got worse. Deep down, I knew something was wrong. I could feel it, like a shadow creeping over our marriage, but I didn't know what it was. And Cindy? She wasn't telling me. She'd deny anything was wrong, but her tone, her distance, it all screamed that she wanted out, even if she wouldn't say it.

What I didn't know at the time was that there was another man sitting next to her during some of those phone calls, silently listening in. His name was Chad, a sailor stationed in Memphis, someone she had known from high school. While I was halfway around the world serving my country, Cindy had rekindled her relationship with him, leaving me alone in more ways than one.

I didn't know about Chad then, though. All I knew was that my marriage was crumbling, and every attempt to fix it felt like pouring water out of a sinking ship. Cindy wouldn't tell me the truth, and I was desperate for answers. One night, out of sheer frustration and helplessness, I did something I never thought I'd do; I hacked into Cindy's email account. I guessed her password on the first try; "Cindyland." It was one of her favorite phrases, and when it worked, I was filled with dread.

My fingers trembled as I went through her inbox. At first, it was just the usual emails, nothing that seemed out of place. But then I saw it, message after message from the same email address; Chad. My heart sank as I opened the first one. The emails were graphic, painfully so, detailing their encounters, their feelings for each other, and their plans for the future. They had been together for months, since Valentine's Day, at least. The word "love" was scattered throughout the emails, a constant reminder that this wasn't just a fling. This was an affair, something deeper, something I had been completely blind to. I printed the emails, unsure what I'd do with them, but knowing they'd eventually come to light in court.

It was April, and I wouldn't be able to confront her until I returned to the States in June. The waiting was torture. A few weeks later, I received divorce papers in the mail, and with them, the last piece of my world crumbled. I had held on to hope, thinking we could fix things, even with Chad in the picture. But the divorce papers shattered that illusion. It didn't seem to matter to Cindy or her attorney that serving divorce papers to a deployed service member was illegal. The judge would later chastise them for it, but at the time, I didn't care. The damage was done. I felt utterly defeated and was placed on suicide watch.

I never had any intention of taking my own life, but I had become a shell of myself. I didn't eat, I didn't sleep; I just existed, completely numb. My command, seeing my deterioration, decided to ship me back to the States early to handle the legal matters at home.

* * *

The flight home felt like the longest journey of my life. Everything I cared about was on the line, and I was left waiting, uncertain about the fate of my young family. Deep down, I knew my marriage was likely over, but what would happen with my daughter? What kind of life would we have now that everything I once held dear had been shattered? The future felt like a void, and I was lost, unsure of what was left or what might come next.

As the plane touched down, I braced myself for the inevitable heartbreak, even though I already knew what was coming. When I arrived at the house, Cindy opened the door, and in that instant, I could see my worst fears confirmed. Her once warm, inviting eyes were now empty, devoid of any love or connection. The woman standing before me looked like my wife, but she wasn't there anymore, she had been taken by a man who should have been thankful for my sacrifice, but instead had stolen my entire world. Even Kim seemed distant, as if a part of her had already slipped away. Cindy had packed up the car before I got there, anticipating my arrival. She loaded Kim into the car, and I stood there, powerless, watching as she packed away everything that had ever mattered to me.

As I watched Cindy drive over the hill with my daughter in the car, it felt like my entire world came crashing down. In that moment, I lost everything that mattered to me. I had gone away to defend their freedom, and in her finally gratitude now here she was taking away my family. It was the most profound betrayal I'd ever experienced. Cindy, the woman I had shared my first intimate moments with, the mother of my child, the person I had given my whole heart to, she was gone. The emotional pain was overwhelming, like being doused in gasoline and set ablaze. Every nerve in my body felt raw, exposed, and throbbed with an agony that seemed unending.

Cindy moved back in with her parents, leaving behind a mess, both in my life and in our marital home that made me question everything I thought I knew about her. The house was unlivable, trash was piled two or three feet high throughout the rooms, with the stench of neglect hanging in the air. It took me over a week to clean up the filth, and as I worked, my heart broke again. How could she have let our daughter live in these conditions?

To compound the emotional harm she had already inflicted upon me, Cindy refused to let me see Kim. My own daughter, who I hadn't held in over six months. I had to wait until our court date, hoping the judge would grant me visitation. I appeared in court, standing next to my attorney, while Cindy and hers sat across from us. My attorney requested temporary visitation, and thankfully, the judge agreed.

I'll never forget that long awaited moment. Finally, after months of heartache and separation, I got to hold my little girl. But the joy was tinged with frustration; frustration that Cindy had made me fight through legal channels just to see my own daughter. I had fought so hard for my country, and now I was battling in court for the right to be a father. Even though the battle was far from over, that first moment with Kim gave me the strength I needed. But deep down, I knew that nothing would ever be the same.

Chapter 60

In the days leading up to the court date, I was consumed by a relentless exhaustion. If it wasn't one of the rare days when I got to see Kim, I spent the entire day sleeping, buried in blankets, trying to escape my despair. It was as if all the energy had drained from my body, leaving me hollow. Normally, I couldn't sleep past six in the morning no matter how hard I tried, but now I couldn't get enough. It was like I was sinking into a black hole, sleeping eighteen, sometimes twenty hours a day. My only breaks were for light meals, and then it was back to sleep, my only refuge from the world that was falling apart around me.

Weeks passed like this, and when I finally started to pull myself out of the darkness, I had a vivid, haunting dream that gripped me in a way few dreams ever had. The events in my nightmare were so compelling that I decided I would write a book about it. For the first time in weeks, I had something to focus on, something that gave me a reason to stay awake. It felt cathartic, almost like I was healing through the writing process.

Every day, I spent ten to twelve hours in front of the computer, the words flowing out of me. What started as a short story quickly expanded into a full-length novel. I named it "The Spirit Among Us". When I finally finished, I printed the whole manuscript and tucked it away in a box. It sat there for years, untouched, until I pulled it out during college and rewrote it. I even managed to sell a few copies along the way, but it wasn't until nearly twenty years later that I would revisit the book and decide to officially publish it. The writing had been a lifeline during the darkest chapter of my life, and now it was a testament to my endurance and overcoming obstacles. My dyslexia was the chief of these problems during the writing process.

* * *

The court date finally arrived. I stood in front of the judge, nervous and prepared, with the printed emails between Cindy and Chad in my hands. Cindy had no choice but to admit to the affair, there was no denying the explicit details laid out in the emails. The evidence was overwhelming. Our marriage was dissolved in that sterile courtroom, and though the court granted us joint custody, primary custody of Kim was given to Cindy. The judge's reasoning infuriated me; I hadn't been in my daughter's life for the past year. As if I had any choice in the matter! I had been deployed, serving my country, and that fact had been completely dismissed.

The outcome crushed me in ways I never thought possible. Losing my marriage had been painful enough, but the idea that my time with Kim would be so limited tore me apart. I was left feeling helpless, powerless to protect the relationship with my daughter. That day in court terrified me in ways I hadn't anticipated, I swore to myself that I would never have another child. If the system could take my daughter away, what was stopping it from happening again with someone else? That fear lodged itself deep inside me, and it would stay with me for years to come, shaping how I approached every relationship thereafter.

* * *

Not long after the divorce I was honorably discharged from the Marine corps, so I packed up my things, loaded them into a U-Haul truck, and began the long, two-thousand-mile journey back home to Washington State. I needed to be with my parents, to rebuild and regain the emotional strength I had lost. I have to admit, without the love and support of my parents, I don't know how I would had made it through this most difficult time in my life. I've always been grateful for them always being there to pick me up when I fell.

As part of the court order, I was supposed to have visitation rights a few times a year and the right to participate in major decisions in Kim's life. But those were just words on paper, and they would soon mean nothing. Cindy wasted no time disregarding the custody agreement. When it was time for me to have my visitation she refused to put Kim on a plane, despite me paying for the ticket. My only recourse would have been to fly down and petition the court, but she knew I didn't have the resources to do this.

She moved, taking Kim out of state with Chad, without telling me a thing. I only found out when her phone was disconnected, and suddenly, I had no way of contacting them; I was furious. The parenting plan clearly stated she wasn't allowed to move Kim out of state without the court's permission, but when I brought it up to the court, they did nothing. It seemed like no one cared what Cindy did, as long as she had custody.

I tried everything I could to maintain some kind of connection with Kim. I sent her a letter every month, hoping one day I'd get a response. But none of my letters were ever answered, and I was left in the dark, with no idea where my daughter was. The only option I had was to hire a good lawyer, but I didn't have the money. I was struggling to get through college, scraping by, barely able to make ends meet, let alone afford an expensive court battle.

In my desperation, I made a terrible decision. Since Cindy wasn't following the court order and the court didn't seem to care, I decided to stop paying child support, hoping that might get her attention. Maybe if the money stopped, she'd reach out, and we could figure something out. But it didn't work. Instead, the state came after me. The Washington courts were notified that I was delinquent in my support payments, and before long, I found myself standing in front of a judge once again.

I told the judge the situation, about how Cindy had disappeared with my daughter, how I hadn't been able to see Kim despite the court's visitation order. I explained that I wasn't trying to avoid my responsibility but that I was desperate to see my child. The judge didn't seem to care. All that appeared to matter was the money. I was threatened with jail time if I didn't keep up with the child support payments, so I paid. Even though I hadn't seen Kim in over a year, even though Cindy had essentially kidnapped her, I paid despite having my rights stripped from me.

Chapter 61

After years of searching, after years of sending letters that went unanswered, I finally gave up any hope of having a part in my daughter's life. The court wouldn't enforce my rights, so it felt like I didn't have any. If I didn't have any rights, I thought, what was the point of holding on? I made the painful decision to sign away my parental rights. Maybe, if I'd had a lawyer or more resources, I could have fought harder. But I was tired; tired of fighting a losing battle, tired of being denied access to my daughter. I still sent letters, though I never heard back from Kim or Cindy. It was as if I had been erased from my daughter's life, and I didn't see her again for fifteen years.

* * *

Immediately following my discharge from the military, I found myself adrift, caught in a space between my past life and the future that had yet to reveal itself. I had no concrete plans, no real direction. Living with my parents wasn't a permanent solution, but beyond that, I had no idea what my next steps would be. I had no clear vision for my career or how I would support myself. It felt like I was floating in limbo, waiting for something, anything, to push me toward a new purpose. Sometimes, destiny has a way of knocking on the door when you least expect it.

One afternoon, as I sat aimlessly trying to figure out my next move, the phone rang. It wasn't a call I was expecting, and when I picked it up, I was surprised to hear my favorite aunt on the other end. Aunt Laurel, and though we didn't speak often, this time there was something in her voice, a kind of excitement that immediately piqued my interest. It was out of the norm for her to call specifically to talk to me, so I listened carefully, wondering what this was about.

"Are you available to perform on the Snow Train?" she asked, cutting straight to the point.

I had no idea what she was talking about, so I asked her to explain. She told me that her travel company organized an annual train ride that took several hundred people from Seattle to Leavenworth for the tree lighting ceremony; a festive journey full of fun and entertainment. The Snow Train was a popular tradition, and this year they were looking for another person to perform magic and entertain the passengers during the trip.

It sounded like an incredible opportunity. I imagined myself performing in front of an audience, doing what I loved, while the train chugged through the snow-covered mountains. It was exactly the kind of adventure I needed, a chance to break out of the limbo I was in and reignite my passion for magic. But there was a catch, in order to be selected for the trip, I had to audition.

Suddenly, the nerves hit. It had been a while since I'd performed for anyone other than a few friends or small gatherings. This was a much bigger deal, and I knew that if I wanted to be chosen, I had to give it my all. But something inside me stirred, maybe it was the Marine in me, or maybe it was just the hope that this opportunity could be the turning point I'd been waiting for. Either way, I decided I was going to take the leap.

"Of course, I'll do it!" I told her, excitement bubbling up in my voice.

We set up a date for the audition, and the days leading up to it were a blur of rehearsals, refining my tricks, and building my confidence back up. I didn't know where this would lead, but for the first time since my discharge, I had a sense of direction, a goal to work toward.

When the day of the audition arrived, I stepped into the room with butterflies in my stomach. But as soon as I started performing, everything fell into place. The nervousness faded, replaced by the joy and focus that always came with performing magic. The small group laughed at the right moments, gasped at the reveals, and I felt that old spark reignite.

After the audition, I waited anxiously for the call that would determine whether or not I'd secured the job. When the phone rang, and I heard my aunt's voice on the other end, I knew this was it.

"You're in," she said.

I felt a wave of relief and excitement wash over me. This was my chance, a door opening when I needed it the most. Little did I know, that single audition would set me on a path that would change my life forever. The Snow Train was just the beginning.

My time on the Snow Train became a yearly tradition, a stage where I could build and refine my performance skills over several years. Each journey through the snowy mountain landscape offered me a new opportunity to grow as an entertainer, and it was here that I honed my stage presence and developed my confidence in front of an audience. The train car, filled with eager passengers, became my classroom, and each show taught me something new about timing, pacing, and how to captivate a crowd.

I quickly learned how to engage with people, how to read an audience, and how to adapt when things didn't go as planned. The intimate setting of the train forced me to think on my feet and gave me an opportunity to experiment with new tricks, routines, and techniques that would later become cornerstones of my act. The passengers, with their excitement and willingness to be entertained, fueled my passion. With every trip, my abilities improved, my confidence grew, and I could feel myself evolving into a true performer.

In many ways, those years on the Snow Train laid the foundation for the performer I am today. The skills I developed, the lessons I learned, and the experience I gained during those journeys were invaluable. They gave me a stage to perfect my craft, and without that crucial period, I know I wouldn't have the same level of comfort and mastery on stage now.

I've always been deeply grateful to my Aunt Laurel and Alki Tours for giving me that chance. They saw something in me, even when I was still trying to figure out my path, and offered me an opportunity that would change my life forever. The Snow Train wasn't just a job, it was the turning point that set me on the road to becoming a professional magician and performer. It gave me the chance to pursue a passion that, at one time, seemed like just a dream. That opportunity wasn't just about earning a paycheck or filling a role, it was about discovering who I was and what I was truly capable of. It shaped the course of my future, and for that, I'll always be thankful.

Chapter 62

My spelling and reading issues continued to plague me even in my college years. While they are distinct subjects, I believe they still go hand in hand. College in general turned out to be much easier than I anticipated. I actually studied for each class, which was something I hadn't needed to do in high school. To be honest, I could have coasted through many of my College subjects by simply taking good notes and completing my homework. I hadn't even opened several of the expensive course books for the class.

That all changed when I enrolled in my first and only calculus class. Calculus was, by far, the hardest class I ever took during my college years. Fortunately for me, I had an ace up my sleeve; my sister, Kristen. She was one of the smartest people I've ever known. At the time, she was a senior in college, while I was just a sophomore. Kristen was studying to become an engineer, and her math courses were several levels above mine. In fact, her coursework was so advanced that I struggled to even understand the questions, let alone try to solve them. Thankfully, Kristen was kind and patient enough to tutor me regularly. I can honestly say that without her help, it would have been nearly impossible for me to achieve my usual "A" in calculus.

One day, while I was working through some calculus homework, I heard a commotion coming from downstairs. My brother, Ted, was yelling, and his voice was grating on my nerves, making it impossible to focus. I tried to ignore him, but eventually, curiosity got the better of me. I decided to head downstairs to see what the problem was.

When I reached the living room, I found Ted shouting at our mom on another one of his countless rants. At first, I was curious about what had set him off this time. Over the years, Ted had become more emotionally unstable, and his outbursts had become increasingly frequent. As I stood there, listening, it became clear that Ted was blaming our mom for all of his problems in life, accusing her of being responsible for his failures.

It didn't take long for me to grow tired of his disrespect toward our mother. At first, Ted ignored me, but he quickly noticed my mood shifting.

"What? What's your problem?" Ted screamed at me, as if I had anything to do with his issues. Then his accusations were suddenly directed in my direction. "It's your fault too!"

That was the last straw. I'd had enough of his tirades. Without thinking, I simply replied, "Waaaahh," mocking his childish complaints.

My response sent Ted into a blind rage. Before I could react, he charged at me with incredible speed. He grabbed me, lifted me over his head, and slammed me onto the floor in a brutal piledriver wrestling move. Pain shot through my spine the moment I hit the ground. For a terrifying second, I thought I might be paralyzed. Thankfully, I could still move, but my shock quickly turned to fury.

Ted could have seriously injured or even killed me with his reckless attack, and I wasn't going to let that slide; not this time. I shot up, looking for something, anything, to use as a weapon. Ted was much bigger and stronger than me and I would need it to defeat him. When I couldn't find anything nearby, I rushed at him in a blind rage. But before I could get to him, my mom stepped between us like an immovable oak tree, preventing what could have been a disastrous fight.

I'm glad she did, because in that moment, my emotions had completely overridden any rational thought. If it weren't for her intervention, I might have hurt Ted badly. I walked away that day, but from that moment on, Ted and I didn't get along. Any semblance of a relationship we had before was destroyed. To me, family doesn't try to kill family, and Ted had crossed an unforgivable line. Perhaps one day we'll be able to mend this fence, but right now it seems like a pipe dream.

Chapter 63

During my time in college, as I began to explore the internet, which was still relatively new back then, I stumbled upon chat rooms that connected people from all over the world. One evening, I found myself chatting with a girl named Penny. She was from Sydney, Australia, and we instantly clicked. Our conversations were lighthearted at first, but soon, our daily email exchanges grew longer and more personal.

We became close friends, and as the months passed, I found myself developing feelings for her, something I never expected from an online interaction. In hindsight, I now realize that I was probably rebounding from the pain of my failed marriage, grasping for anything that resembled love or connection.

As the school year neared its end, and with summer break just around the corner, we made a bold decision; I would fly to Australia to meet her in person. I was both excited and nervous, but the idea of seeing Penny after months of emails and conversations made the long flight bearable. I bought my ticket, made all the necessary arrangements, and embarked on the longest journey of my life.

When I landed in Sydney, the airport felt overwhelming. I walked around the luggage area, our agreed-upon meeting spot, but I didn't see Penny anywhere. Panic started to set in. Had I flown halfway across the world just to be stood up? My mind raced through the worst-case scenarios, where would I stay if she didn't show up? I hadn't made any backup plans.

After wandering around for over an hour, I finally spotted her, sitting quietly in a corner as if she had been watching me the whole time. Relief washed over me, but a small part of me wondered why she hadn't approached me earlier. Still, she greeted me with a smile, and her brother helped carry my bags. We took the train to her town, and after what felt like another eternity, we arrived at her home.

That first night was awkward. We slept in separate beds, both in the same room, and spent hours talking, catching up on everything we hadn't been able to say over email. Eventually, Penny invited me to join her in her bed; I hesitated. My heart had been broken before, and I promised myself I would take things slow. But she coaxed me gently, and my longing for love, my shattered heart won over. I needed to feel cared for, to be loved again. So, I joined her.

The next evening, there was a knock on the door. Penny answered it, and a man walked in as if he owned the place. His name was Neil, and he introduced himself as Penny's "on-again, off-again" boyfriend. I was stunned. She hadn't mentioned Neil in any of our emails or conversations. My stomach churned with dread. The following night, Neil and Penny spent the night together in her bedroom while I lay on the couch, staring at the ceiling, my heart breaking for the second time in my life.

It was only my second day in Australia, and I was already miserable. I couldn't believe how quickly everything had unraveled. A few days later, Penny sat me down with a somber expression and revealed that she was pregnant. She showed me her test results, confirming that she had been pregnant for at least a month; long before I'd arrived. She admitted that Neil was the father. It was too much for me to bear.

I knew I needed to leave, but I didn't have many options. Luckily, I found a kind family who agreed to take me in for a few weeks. They were generous, but their beliefs were…different. They had some unusual ideas about life, and I found myself tiptoeing around certain subjects. One evening, I made the mistake of mentioning that I believed there could be life on other planets. To them, that was blasphemous. They immediately placed their hands on me and began praying that God would "purge my mind of these impure thoughts." I tried not to offend them, but after that incident, it became clear I had overstayed my welcome.

Reluctantly, I returned to Penny's house for a few days until I could change my flight home. While I was there, I noticed several messages from other men on her computer. It became obvious that Penny was stringing along multiple guys, not just me and Neil. Seeing those messages cemented my decision to leave as quickly as possible. I changed my flight to the next day and boarded the plane back to the States, feeling utterly defeated.

I had come to Australia searching for love, hoping to find solace after a broken marriage, but instead, I had found more heartache. As the plane soared into the sky, I realized I needed to learn how to heal on my own before seeking love in someone else again.

Chapter 64

A year had passed since I finished my first degree in psychology. With a diploma in hand, I stood at a crossroads, unsure of what to do next. My love for understanding the human mind had carried me through school, but now, as I looked ahead, the future seemed hazy. Unsure of what path to take, I decided to enroll in a new program, this time in criminal justice. I figured it couldn't hurt to explore a different field, and maybe the structured world of law and order would provide the clarity I was seeking.

The criminal justice degree came quickly, faster than I expected. With my new qualifications, I made the decision to become a cop. The idea excited me at first. There was something empowering about serving the community, being on the front lines, and making a real difference. I threw myself into the process, taking tests, going through interviews, and feeling more confident with each step.

But the night before my final interview, something unsettling happened. I had a vivid dream, one that felt more like a premonition than just a trick of my subconscious. In the dream, I was patrolling the streets when I pulled over a teenager. He looked nervous, too nervous for just a routine traffic stop.

Somehow, I knew, deep in my gut, that he had weed stashed in his glove compartment. I calmly asked him to open it, expecting nothing more than a few grams of marijuana. But instead of cooperating, he pulled out a gun. Without warning, he shot me in the chest multiple times. I could feel the searing pain as I fell to the ground, paralyzed and helpless, watching as he sped off into the night, leaving me there to die alone on the asphalt.

I woke up drenched in sweat, the image of that dream replaying in my mind. The clarity of it, the intensity; it shook me to my core. I couldn't shake the feeling that it was more than just a dream, that it was some kind of warning. As I lay in bed, wide-eyed and anxious, I decided that I couldn't go through with the final interview. The dream had rattled me too much, and I wasn't about to tempt fate.

To make matters worse, the girl I was dating at the time gave me an ultimatum; if I became a cop, she would break up with me. It felt like the universe was conspiring to keep me away from law enforcement. Between the dream and the fear of losing her, I made my decision; I wouldn't become a cop.

With my law enforcement ambitions in the rearview mirror, I looked toward another familiar path, one my father had walked before me. He had built a successful career as an electrician, and I figured I could follow in his footsteps. I decided to become an electrical apprentice, diving headfirst into the trade. The work was demanding, both mentally and physically, but I liked the challenge. There was a certain satisfaction in working with my hands, in understanding how things were wired together, and in making sure everything functioned safely.

* * *

The days were long, filled with school and on-the-job training, but I never let go of my passion for performing. On the weekends, I transformed from an electrician to a magician and hypnotist, performing at events whenever I could. There was something exhilarating about being on stage, captivating an audience with illusions and mind-bending tricks. The dual life I was leading, electrician by day, performer by night, kept me on my toes. It wasn't easy to juggle both, but I thrived on the challenge.

Despite my busy schedule, I still found time for one of my favorite pastimes; dancing. Whenever I could, I would hit the dance floor, losing myself in the rhythm and forgetting, for a while, about the heavy workload that awaited me the next day. Life, though hectic, had a balance. I was working hard, performing, and living in the moment. And for the first time in a long time, I felt like I was exactly where I was meant to be.

Chapter 65

At this point in my life, I know I'm probably starting to sound like a broken record. And truth be told, I was a slow learner when it came to romantic relationships. Back then, online dating sites didn't exist, and the internet was still growing, so my options for meeting women were limited. My main outlet for meeting someone was dancing, and despite my best intentions, I kept going back to the same place, hoping that one day I'd meet a nice girl. Of course, that never happened.

But I did meet Red. Red was a fiery redhead with a personality to match, and she was obsessed with the newly-released Harry Potter series. Every time a new book came out, she'd buy it, devour it, and be hungry for more. Red worked in the medical field and wore scrubs every day, and after a few nights of dancing together, we quickly became inseparable, spending most of our free time together. It wasn't long before we became boyfriend and girlfriend, and the of course we eventually got engaged. But even as the excitement grew, my instincts began to tingle. Something wasn't right.

Over time, I discovered Red was in serious financial trouble; over $20,000 in debt, and collection agents were hounding her daily. I stepped in to help, arranging to pay off her debt with a loan from my father, and Red signed a contract promising to repay us both. But this financial issue was just the beginning of our problems.

One day, a man who also frequented the dance club with us stopped by her house while I was there waiting for her. He had a reputation for being a player, and the way he acted around Red set off alarm bells. His familiarity with her, the way he moved and spoke, it was like he thought he was her fiancé, not me. He seemed surprised to find me there and quickly made an excuse to leave, but the interaction left me suspicious. I had been betrayed before, and I didn't want to believe it was happening again, but it was hard to shake the feeling. It wasn't until a few months after the relationship ended, I discovered that this man had been fooling around with Red. This was confirmed by the man's then girlfriend who confronted me on the subject.

As the tension between Red and me grew, so did her temper. She was a trained kickboxer, and when she got angry, she didn't hesitate to use her training on me. Every time she hit me, I was both impressed by her strength and frustrated by her lack of control. For someone so small, she could hit harder than some of the Marines I'd boxed with. Just to be clear, I never hit her back; ever.

I knew things were escalating, and one day, during a heated argument, I could see the storm brewing. I decided to walk away to avoid another fight, but as I turned, I saw something coming toward me; fast. Before I could react, her fist connected with my jaw, harder than I'd ever been hit in my life, and I'd taken plenty of punches. My legs buckled beneath me, and I crumpled to the floor in a daze, barely able to stand. The force of her punch had left me stunned, and it was several minutes before I could even get back on my feet.

Red stormed off without a single shred of remorse. She'd crossed the line long ago, and I'd had enough. I called the police. When the officers arrived, Red immediately played the victim, claiming I had attacked her, dragged her around the house by her wrist. But the officers could clearly see the mark on my face, a bright red bruise from her punch. Two of the cops believed me, but the sergeant in charge was skeptical. He came over to me and gave me an ominous warning.

"If it wasn't for my two subordinates talking me out of it, I'd be arresting you right now. Count your lucky stars," he said coldly.

Despite his threats, they arrested Red. As they led her out in tears, she was taken to the hospital instead of jail, where she was diagnosed with bipolar disorder and put on medication. Not long after that, Red broke off the engagement. In retrospect, I should have been the one to end it first, but I was worried that if I left, she'd refuse to repay the loan she owed my dad and me.

My fears were realized when Red stopped making payments. The money was significant enough that I hired a lawyer to try and recover the funds, but Red filed for bankruptcy, freeing her from her financial obligations. It was a harsh and painful lesson, one I never forgot. Though I had lost the money, the emotional cost was far greater. I learned that some people can charm you with sweet words and promises, but when the mask falls, it can leave scars much deeper than financial ruin.

Chapter 66

Meeting Mandy was like a whirlwind. We clicked almost immediately. She was beautiful, with an infectious smile, and she could dance like nobody I'd ever seen. We met at a club one night, and from the first dance, I was hooked. It wasn't long before we started dating, and before I knew it, we were living together. It was strange for me, I'd never lived with a woman before unless I was married to her. But everything seemed to be moving fast, and within a few months, we were engaged.

Meeting her parents came next. They lived in a beautiful house, and her father was clearly successful, working for an electrical contractor. Her mother, always warm at first, took a keen interest in my background, especially my faith.

"Are you a Mormon, Joe?" her mother asked over dinner, her eyes studying me carefully.

I glanced at Mandy, then back at her mother. "No, I'm Christian."

Her expression changed. I could tell immediately that this wasn't the answer she was hoping for. The rest of the evening carried on, but the tension had settled in the air.

Later that night, on the drive home, Mandy broke the silence.

"They like you," she started. "But... they're concerned that you're not Mormon."

"Is that going to be a problem?" I asked, trying to hide the apprehension I felt growing inside me.

She hesitated. "I don't think so, but... it would help if you converted to Mormonism."

I looked at her, trying to gauge how serious she was. "I don't think that's something I can do."

Her disappointment was clear, though she tried to play it off. "Well, it's no big deal. I'm sure it'll be fine."

But I wasn't so sure. A few weeks later, we went to a party hosted by a mutual friend named Joel, a guy who frequented the same club where Mandy and I had met. The party was a typical gathering; drinks, music, and lots of dancing. We got separated at some point, and after about half an hour, I realized I hadn't seen Mandy in a while.

Worried, I started looking for her. As I approached the top of the spiral staircase, I froze. Below, at the bottom of the steps, I saw her talking to Joel. My heart sank as I watched her lean in and kiss him. It wasn't just a friendly peck, it was intimate, far too familiar. And then she looked up and saw me standing there. The guilt was written all over her face.

I walked down the stairs in silence, my emotions in turmoil. I passed them without saying a word and headed straight for the door. I could hear her calling after me.

"Joel, where are you going?"

She even got my name wrong.

"Home," I replied coldly.

"What about me?"

"I'm sure Joel can give you a ride home," I said, not even turning to look at her.

I drove home alone, angry and heartbroken. But as much as I wanted to walk away, I couldn't just leave her stranded. Eventually, I went back, let her into the car, and drove her home. Once we reached the apartment, I made sure she was safe inside and then left again, retreating to my parents' house, my place of refuge.

The next day, Mandy showed up at our parents' house, begging for forgiveness. I loved her, and against my better judgment, I tried to forgive her. But trust, once broken, is hard to rebuild. She tried to make things better for a while, but it didn't last. She stopped helping around the house, didn't contribute to rent or groceries, and quit her job altogether. My patience was wearing thin. She talked about finding work but instead landed a part in a local play.

Curious to see her in action, I decided to surprise her at one of the rehearsals. When I arrived, I saw her in the arms of the play's director. The embrace was far too intimate for comfort, and the moment she saw me, she pulled away, making excuses about it being part of the performance. But my trust in her had already been shaken. A few days later, she dropped a bombshell; she was pregnant.

It should have been a moment of joy, but instead, I was filled with doubt. The image of her with the director and the memory of her kiss with Joel haunted me. We argued endlessly for the next week, the tension between us unbearable. Eventually, I walked out, needing some air and space to think. But when I returned, Mandy was gone.

She left me a note; Don't bother coming after me. Leave me alone.

And just like that, she was gone, taking our unborn child with her. I was devastated. I went to her parents' house, hoping for answers, but they shut me out, telling me Mandy didn't want to see me. I begged, pleaded for her to come back, to let us work things out, but she ignored every effort I made.

I was desperate to be part of my child's life. I didn't want to be just some absent father, completely shut out from my own child's birth. Months passed with the constant rejection from her entire family I was left with little options. Without any other avenues, I started calling hospitals, trying to find out when my child was born. After weeks of calling, I finally got the news I was waiting for, my son had been born. His name was Simon, a name Mandy had chosen without me. History seemed to be repeating itself.

I filed a paternity case in court and was eventually granted visitation rights. The first time I saw Simon, he was already several months old. He was bigger than I imagined, and it hurt knowing I had missed so much already. My visitation was restricted to four hours every other weekend, an insult, as if I was some kind of criminal with limited access to my own son.

Mandy made everything difficult. One time, she called the cops because I was five minutes late dropping Simon off. She nitpicked every detail of my time with him, what I fed him, where I took him, even how often I checked his diaper. Our relationship, already broken, descended into constant fighting. I wanted to be there for my son, but every step of the way, Mandy tried to push me out. It felt like a losing battle, one I was determined not to give up. But the road ahead was anything but easy.

Chapter 67

Mandy was ordered by the court not to leave the state with our child, so she did the next best thing to make things hard on me. She moved as far away as she could within Washington, all the way to Spokane, over four hours away from where we had been living. She had no job, no money to afford an apartment, and no real reason to be there other than to make it harder for me to see Simon.

The only reason she could afford the move was thanks to her wealthy parents. They didn't approve of me, mainly because I refused to convert to Mormonism. Spokane offered her nothing, no support network, no friends, but none of that mattered. The only thing that did matter was that it made visitation for me a logistical nightmare.

I refused to let the distance keep me from my son. Every visitation, I made the long drive, even though it left me exhausted. Every time I saw Simon was worth the effort, but the tension with Mandy grew unbearable. Every visit turned into a shouting match, with raised voices and bitter arguments. It was so bad that even her parents started acting as mediators to ease the tension. I thought things might improve, that over time we'd find a way to co-parent peacefully, but instead, things just got worse.

The constant stress began taking a toll on my health. I started experiencing severe panic attacks, chest pains, and chronic anxiety. Every day, I felt like I was on the verge of a heart attack. My nights were restless, my body constantly on edge. I was a wreck, physically and emotionally, barely holding myself together. I didn't know how much longer I could keep going like this.

Eventually, my doctor gave me a harsh wake-up call. "You need to make a change," he told me. "This stress is killing you. If you don't do something soon, it's going to get a lot worse."

That's when I realized something had to give. The constant fighting with Mandy, the strained visits, the hostility, it wasn't just affecting me. It was poisoning everything, even my time with Simon. I didn't want my son to grow up on a battleground, with two parents constantly at each other's throats. He deserved better than that. But at the same time, I felt trapped. I wanted to be there for him, but the situation had become toxic, and I didn't know how to fix it.

After weeks of agonizing over the decision, I did something I still struggle with to this day, I decided to allow Mandy's parents to adopt Simon. It was a decision born out of desperation and exhaustion. I convinced myself it would be better for everyone, especially my son. Maybe it was a selfish choice. Maybe it was a mistake. But at the time, I didn't see any other way out. I was drowning in the stress, and I couldn't bear the thought of dragging Simon through years of this conflict.

I tell myself now that if I could go back, I'd make a different choice. That I wouldn't give up, that I'd fight harder. But in that moment, all I wanted was peace, peace for my son, peace for myself, peace for everyone involved. I had no idea what the long-term consequences would be, and to this day, it remains one of the hardest decisions I've ever made.

Chapter 68

After the pain of losing two children in different ways, I made a decision that felt irreversible at the time; I got a vasectomy. It was a choice born from deep wounds. I couldn't bear the thought of risking that kind of heartache again. I was still young, and many people would have said I had my whole life ahead of me, but to me, the idea of fatherhood had become a painful prospect.

The scars from those experiences ran too deep. I thought about how I'd failed, how I couldn't imagine giving up another child, and it felt like the right decision. The panic attacks and stress that had plagued me finally started to fade, but the emotional pain lingered like a dull ache that never fully went away.

In an effort to move forward, I found solace in the dance clubs. Dancing had always been an escape for me, a way to lose myself in the music and forget about everything else for a while. It became my distraction from the void in my life. One night, though, something unexpected happened.

As I stood on the edge of the dance floor, I noticed a woman who immediately caught my eye. She was stunning, the kind of beautiful that made your heart skip a beat. Watching her move with such grace and confidence, I couldn't help but think, "Why can't I get someone like that?" She seemed so out of reach, like someone in a completely different league. But dancing, that was something I could do. Maybe, just maybe, she'd be willing to share a dance with me.

I gathered my nerve and approached her. "Would you like to dance?" I asked, fully expecting her to decline.

To my surprise, she smiled and said yes. Her name was Anna. We danced for hours, and as the night went on, I realized that we were hitting it off. She was warm, friendly, and seemed to be enjoying my company just as much as I was enjoying hers. It was the first time in a long while that I felt something like hope. When the night was winding down, I pushed my luck and asked for her number. I nearly couldn't believe it when she gave it to me.

* * *

A few days later, I worked up the courage to call her and asked her out on a proper date. She agreed, and we went to the movies. The whole evening felt surreal. After the movie, I felt a surge of boldness and leaned in to kiss her. To my amazement, she kissed me back. It wasn't long before we planned another date, and then another, until we were spending all of our free time together. Before I knew it, we were a couple.

Anna was everything I had ever dreamed of in a woman. She was beautiful, driven, and had a solid job. She was working on getting her Bachelor's degree and had ambitions for the future. On top of all that, she was athletic and loved sports, a perfect match for me in so many ways. People at the dance club would tell me she was out of my league, that there was no way we'd last. But for the first time in a long time, I didn't care what anyone else thought. I had found someone who made me feel alive again.

We hadn't officially moved in together, but it felt like we had. I spent almost every night at her place, leaving from there for work in the mornings. I was working with my dad at the time, learning the ropes as an electrician, and things seemed to be going well for me in all aspects of my life. It was the first time in years that I felt like I had a future to look forward to. With Anna by my side, it felt like maybe, just maybe, I could heal from the past and build something new.

* * *

Joining Anna's co-ed soccer team seemed like a great way to bond, even though I'd never played on an organized soccer team before. I was fast, probably one of the fastest players on the team, but I lacked the experience the others had. I made mistakes, more than I'd like to admit, but I was improving. I even managed to score a few goals, which felt like an incredible achievement.

But then came the last game I'd ever play, a game that would change everything. It was the final play I'd ever make, a nearly perfect pass came my way. I was onside, and as soon as the ball passed me, I surged forward. It was just me and the goalkeeper now, the ball still a few yards ahead, but within reach. I glanced over my shoulder, ensuring no defenders were closing in. When I turned back to the ball, I saw a shadow from the other side. Before I could react, the goalkeeper collided with me at full speed.

The impact was brutal. I felt pain explode through my body, and we both crumpled to the ground. I knew immediately something was wrong, but I refused to acknowledge the severity. The goalkeeper went to the hospital; I, stubborn as always, did not. Even though I could barely stand, I convinced myself it was nothing serious and limped off the field with help.

What I didn't realize at the time was that I had shattered my knee. Without surgery, it would never fully heal, and it became a permanent injury that would remind me for the rest of my life of my youthful stubbornness. I can still walk without a limp, but I'll never be able to run the way I used to.

Chapter 69

A few months later, everything else in my life began to crumble, just as people had predicted. Anna broke things off with me, seemingly out of nowhere. It hit me hard, like a sucker punch I hadn't seen coming. In the back of my mind, I'd always feared she was out of my league. Maybe that was why I went out of my way to make her happy. Flowers, thoughtful gestures, she was always my top priority. But maybe she thought I was beneath her, that I didn't match up to the life she envisioned. A few weeks later, she called me, asking to come back, and like the fool I did. I still loved her, after all.

We tried again, but it didn't last. A few months later, she ended things again. This time, the pain was just as intense, if not worse. I tried to bury myself in work, but nothing could distract me from the emptiness I felt. Coming home to my condo, day after day, with nothing but silence and memories of what we had; it was soul-crushing.

Then, just when I had started to adjust, my phone rang. I was shocked to hear her voice. Anna missed me, she said. She wanted me back. Stupidly, I said yes again. I didn't want to lose her, so I proposed. Much to my surprise, she accepted. But a few weeks later, she called off the engagement, saying she wasn't ready for marriage yet. I could feel her slipping away again, and no matter what I did, I couldn't stop it.

One day, after a long day at work, I came back to Anna's place, but my key didn't work. I tried over and over, thinking it was just a mistake. When I couldn't get in, I squeezed through the slightly open garage door she left for her cat. Something felt off. As I entered our room, I saw a stuffed heart hanging from the ceiling over her bed. It hadn't been there before.

"That's strange," I muttered, reaching for it.

Attached was a note in someone else's handwriting, a man's handwriting; it was a love note. My heart sank. I found another note on the nightstand, confirming my worst fears; Anna had been cheating on me. I called her at work, but she refused to talk about it, only telling me I wasn't welcome at her place anymore. She had changed the locks, and I hadn't even known.

I packed up my things, feeling utterly defeated. I was done. This time, there was no going back. I couldn't stay somewhere I wasn't wanted, and I wasn't going to tolerate being cheated on. As I drove away, I was left with the familiar ache of failure. I spent the next few years trying to figure out what I had done wrong, why I seemed to pick women who couldn't stay faithful. The truth, though, was that I just kept choosing the wrong people. Unfortunately, I was a slow learner. The dance clubs that had once been my escape became the place where more trouble waited for me, and I went right back to it.

* * *

In the wake of all these losses, I realized it was time to prioritize myself. I needed to do something special, something I had never done before, as a way to finally take care of my own needs. I had saved up my money because I wanted a reliable vehicle for once.

All my previous cars were used and came with their own issues. This time, I was determined to get something free of those headaches.

I searched long and hard, waiting for the right car at the right price. Finally, everything aligned, and I found the perfect car for me. Driving it off the lot, brand new, felt like a major milestone, I was filled with pride as I took it home for the first time. I made sure to take great care of it. I changed the oil regularly, kept it clean inside and out, and vacuumed it often. It was my pride and joy, and there was something special about being its first and only owner. For the first time, I had something that wasn't worn out by someone else, it was mine from the start, and it felt incredible. Unfortunately, I wouldn't keep if for very long.

Chapter 70

A year later, I met Jan, and if I could change just one thing in my life, meeting her might be the choice I'd make. At first, she treated me incredibly well. Almost immediately, she opened up about her violent ex-husband, a man who, according to her, had once put a gun to her head and threatened to kill her. She told me how he had thrown her down a flight of stairs and nearly killed her. She had a restraining order on him and possession of his home despite only having been married to the man for about a month.

Maybe it was the Marine in me, but something clicked, I felt a deep, instinctual need to protect her. I suppose this might have been her plan the entire time, I was unaware that she had played this game several times before. She was just finishing up her divorce when we started dating, and she had a teenage son still living with her. Normally, I tried to avoid dating women with kids. I'd already seen too much drama around shared custody, and it wasn't something I wanted to deal with. It was a very sensitive subject with me and brought up too many bad memories. But Jan was different, charming, captivating, and I broke my own rule, continuing to see her.

Her divorce wrapped up surprisingly fast, and soon she was officially free. Not long after, she confided that she needed to move. She told me her ex-husband was dangerous, that if he found her, he'd kill her. Without hesitation, I offered her my place, at first as a temporary solution. It was too soon for her to move in, but the thought of her being hurt was unbearable. A temporary solution quickly became permanent. Jan cooked, cleaned, and made me incredible lunches, and best of all, she could dance. She was also brilliant, and I've always been attracted to smart women. I began to think I might have found someone I could spend my life with.

Despite her brief marriage, Jan somehow ended up with a lot of her ex's belonging, his computer, a large-screen TV, and several pieces of furniture. I should've found it more suspicious than I did. But I was blinded by my need to feel loved, and Jan was good at convincing people of anything. She played the victim card often, and it worked on me. I saw myself as her protector, her knight in shining armor. For the most part, she treated me well, but there were a few moments that made my gut churn.

One incident, in particular, stood out. When Jan moved in, we didn't have room for all of her extra furniture. She told me she was going to give some of it to a guy from the dance club we frequented. She wanted to drop it off at his place, and immediately, my instincts flared. I didn't know this guy, and something about the situation set off alarm bells. But I went along with it, wanting to trust her.

When we arrived, the guy was ready to help us unload the furniture, and we moved it inside. That's when things got strange. Jan seemed overly interested in chatting with him outside, admiring his motorcycle. It wasn't just the conversation, it was the familiarity between them, the way he knew intimate details about her life, things I didn't even know. It felt like he was holding back because I was there. When he offered to give her a ride on his bike, she eagerly accepted. But when she saw the look on my face, she hesitated, then declined, sensing the tension.

On the way home, we got into a heated argument. My suspicion had boiled over, and things escalated quickly. I'd had enough, and when we hit a stop sign, I opened the car door, intending to walk the rest of the way home. We weren't far from my condo, and I needed the space to cool off. But Jan wasn't having it. She stepped on the gas just as I was stepping out, trying to stop me from leaving. Thankfully, she didn't hit me, but she sped off, whipping around the corner in a fit of anger.

I started running home, frustrated and angry, unaware that just moments later, her reckless driving had caused a minor accident. It was only a fender bender, but it was a sign, one I didn't fully recognize at the time. No one was hurt, but her temper, her unpredictability, was something I should've paid more attention to.

As our relationship continued, I couldn't shake the feeling that there was more beneath the surface than I understood. And as much as I wanted to be her protector, I was beginning to wonder if Jan was someone I could even save, or if she was someone who would eventually drag me down.

* * *

After the dust had settled from our last blowup, Jan started pressuring me relentlessly to marry her. I wasn't convinced our relationship was strong enough to warrant taking that step, but that didn't stop her from trying. She was persistent, sweetening the deal by pampering me constantly, making it hard to keep my resolve. It's funny how memory can blur when you're being showered with attention.

I found myself thinking, "If this is what marriage will be like, why not?" But part of me still wondered why she was in such a rush.

Eventually, I caved, agreeing to get married, but I insisted on a prenuptial agreement. Jan didn't like the idea one bit, but she seemed to shrug it off at first. A few weeks later, I handed her the prenup to sign, but she quickly set it aside, saying she'd get to it later. As the wedding date approached, she still hadn't signed it. On the day of our wedding, she hadn't even touched the document. I told her flatly that there would be no wedding unless she signed it. That triggered a huge argument. She threw a fit but begrudgingly signed the document and stormed off to the venue.

With the legal matters finally behind us, I got dressed and headed for the wedding. I didn't take long to get ready, so I was one of the first to arrive. When I got there, my dad looked surprised.

"What's going on with you two?" he asked, a concerned expression on his face.

"What are you talking about?" I asked, puzzled.

"Jan said you weren't coming to the wedding."

I was taken aback. "I never said that. Where is she?"

"She's getting dressed but keeps insisting it's a waste of time because you're not going to show up."

I figured she was still angry from earlier, so I brushed it off. Despite the drama, the wedding went ahead as planned, and for a while, things seemed fine. But that bliss didn't last long.

Chapter 71

Dancing was where Jan and I first connected, so we spent many nights out on the dance floor together. One evening, my brother Ted joined us, an invitation I later learned had come from Jan. At the time, I didn't think much of it, but that night took on a different meaning soon after.

During a slow, intimate dance, Jan asked Ted to join her on the floor. Ted felt a bit awkward but didn't want to refuse and make her uncomfortable. While they danced, Jan hinted that she wanted to be with him, suggesting they should hook up. Outraged, Ted left her on the dance floor and came straight to me with the story. Shocked, I confronted Jan. She brushed it off, claiming Ted had misunderstood her. Ted had a tendency to exaggerate at times, and I didn't want to believe that Jan would betray me especially with my own brother, so I did my best to take her side, though doubts still lingered.

Later, neighbors informed me that a man had been visiting Jan while I was away. The rumors gnawed at my trust, but with no concrete proof, I chose again to believe Jan. The rumors didn't end there however, my best man confided that Jan had made advances toward him, too. His cryptic account left me feeling uneasy, as though things had gone further than he let on. Trust between Jan and me was eroding quickly, leaving a deep uncertainty that I couldn't shake.

* * *

A month into our marriage, I was watching a Seahawk game, trying to unwind on the couch. Jan was in the kitchen, making lunch, but suddenly decided it was the perfect time to start an argument. She wanted to discuss something trivial, but was being extremely aggressive about it, like she was trying to pick a fight, and I wasn't in the mood to get into it right then. I tried repeatedly to get to to let this go, but she refused to let up. I turned up the volume on the TV, hoping she'd let it go. Instead, she stormed over and unplugged the television.

"Seriously?" I said, trying to keep my cool. "Can we talk after the game?"

She refused, keeping her hold on the TV plug. Frustrated, I decided I'd watch the game somewhere else. I headed to the bedroom to grab my keys and wallet, but as I reached into the dresser drawer, she ran in, slamming her hip into the drawer, pinching my hand inside. The pain shot up my arm. I checked my hand to see if it was broken. I needed my hands for work and performing magic, an injury could cost me thousands of dollars.

"What the hell are you doing?" I shouted, my hand throbbing in pain.

"You're not leaving," she snapped, glaring at me.

"Oh, I'm leaving now," I said, more determined than ever. I walked toward the front door, but before I could leave, Jan blocked my path.

"You're not going anywhere," she growled.

I tried to keep my patience, but she was pushing me too far. When I noticed my wallet and keys were unguarded, I made a run for the bedroom. As soon as I reached for them, Jan tackled me from behind with all her strength, throwing her weight against me and taking me down. I couldn't believe it, she was so small, yet here she was, knocking me off my feet.

I stood back up and tried to open the dresser drawer again, but she leaned against it, using her hip to hold it closed. I tugged on the drawer, and she screamed like I had hurt her, though I knew I hadn't. I released the drawer, knowing it wasn't worth fighting over, and headed for the door again. This time, she jumped onto my back, clawing at me like a wild animal. I ignored the pain, making my way to the door, but she wedged herself against the doorframe, blocking my exit.

"If you don't move, you might fall," I warned, keeping my voice steady.

"You're not leaving!" she screamed in my ear.

I had no choice. I walked through the door, and she lost her grip, tumbling to the ground. I didn't look back as I headed to a bar across the street, figuring she'd cool down by the time the game was over.

* * *

When I returned home later that evening, I was hoping we could talk things out. Instead, I was greeted by a strange, knowing grin on Jan's face. Something was off.

"We can do this the easy way or the hard way," she said cryptically.

"What are you talking about?" I asked, baffled.

As I stepped into the living room, her son hung up the phone, and moments later, I heard the front door slam open.

"Police!" a woman's voice shouted.

I turned to see two officers, one male, one female, storm into the house. My stomach sank.

"Joseph?" the female officer asked.

"Yes?"

"Put your hands on the wall!" she ordered.

I complied, and they spun me around, pushing me against the wall. Before I knew it, I was in handcuffs, being led out of my own home like a criminal, paraded in front of my neighbors. They put me in the back of the patrol car and started asking questions. I told them Jan had attacked me, but they weren't listening. They said she had accused me of assault, and I was under arrest for domestic violence.

When they handed me the statement to sign, I noticed it read like a confession. I told them it didn't reflect what I had just told them. They allowed me to start making revisions to the statement, but they cut me off before I could finish making the corrections. Since they wouldn't let me revise it, I refused to sign.

I spent that night in jail, feeling more humiliated than ever before. Sitting next to convicted murders and rapists for an entire day made me feel more uneasy than I even have felt before in my life. The guards treated me like I was already guilty, though I hadn't been convicted of anything. The psychological toll was heavy, and I wondered how things had spiraled so far out of control. I was innocent, but sitting in that cell, it didn't feel like it mattered.

The harsh reality of jail set in almost immediately. One of the first things I noticed was the so-called "beds" they expected us to sleep on. It wasn't really a bed at all, more like a cold, hard, flat surface with a super thin pad on top. The pad, maybe a quarter of an inch thick, wasn't long enough for me to stretch out on comfortably, and I'm not even a tall guy. My feet hung off the edge, and the tiny blanket they provided wasn't much larger than the pad itself. I was freezing the entire time, and I wondered how anyone could sleep under such conditions. It didn't take long to realize that people could easily get sick just from being in here.

I sat on that so-called bed for hours, in shock and unable to think straight. My mind was stuck on the fact that my life had taken such a drastic and terrifying turn. As I sat there, I heard someone across the room shouting.

"My hand is broken! I need a doctor!" The incarcerated man clutched his hand, yelling for help over and over again.

He screamed for what felt like an eternity, at least an hour, maybe more. Eventually, the small fortified door to the room opened, and several officers in riot gear stormed in, batons raised, shouting for everyone to move back. They rushed the man who'd been yelling, slammed him onto the hard concrete floor with brutal force, and began beating him as he screamed in agony. The sight horrified me. After a few minutes of this violent scene, the man stopped moving. He could have been unconscious maybe worse, I wasn't sure, but they dragged his limp body out of the room. I never saw him again. The brutality and shear uncaring demeanor of the guards was overwhelming.

Fear took over every part of me. I couldn't eat. I couldn't sleep. All I could do was sit there, shivering in the cold, feeling like my world had completely unraveled. They gave us a brown bag for each meal, usually containing a dry bologna sandwich. No mayo, no mustard, no cheese; just bread and some cheap imitation meat. Since I couldn't stomach anything, the guy next to me who said he'd killed someone offered to protect me if I gave him my sandwich. I figured it was better than letting it go to waste, so I handed it over. I spent the next twenty-six hours in that jail, not eating or sleeping the entire time. It was one of the most traumatic experiences of my life.

The nightmare didn't end when I got out. Over the next four months, I fought the domestic violence charge with my attorney. Although I had appeared in court a few times, we never went to trial. In the end, the judge dropped the charges, citing a lack of evidence. I could have told them that from the start. I never laid a finger on Jan, and there were no marks on her to prove otherwise.

What frustrated me most was that they never looked into charging Jan for attacking me or for filing a false report. It seemed like there was no interest in holding her accountable. I was ready to divorce her the moment I walked out of that jail, but somehow, she managed to talk me out of it. I have to admit, she had a silver tongue, she could twist a situation and make you believe it wasn't as bad as it seemed. But the reality was, I didn't feel safe around her anymore.

I had to protect myself. I told Jan that I was installing an internal surveillance system in the condo. I didn't trust being alone with her, and if she ever tried pulling something like that again, I needed proof to protect myself. This time, if the police came, I would have video evidence to show what really happened.

Chapter 72

The stress at home had reached unbearable levels, and it was starting to manifest physically. I began to experience intense anxiety, and the sleepless nights only made it worse. I've always been against going to the doctor, unless I was on my deathbed, it just wasn't something I did. But Jan, insistent as ever, pressured me to seek help; reluctantly, I agreed. The doctor prescribed several medications, promising they'd eventually relieve my symptoms. Weeks passed, yet I felt no relief. He assured me it would just take time, but he couldn't have been more wrong. The medications only made things worse.

* * *

Months later, Jan dropped another bombshell. She told me she was moving back to Arizona, with or without me. I was blindsided. I couldn't just uproot my life. Washington was my home, my family, my job, my schooling. I wasn't prepared to leave everything behind for her, not with the growing distance between us. In my mind, we were heading for a breakup, but Jan, with her silver tongue, once again convinced me otherwise. I still don't know how she did it, but once again, I found myself persuaded to follow her. If I knew what was about to happen I would have never followed her to Arizona.

Against my better judgment, we packed everything up and moved to Arizona. Every fiber of my being screamed that this was a mistake, and I now wish I had listened. Barely a few weeks had passed, and everything changed. Jan started sleeping on the couch, avoiding any physical contact with me. She came home late from work, and when she was home, she barely spoke to me. I had moved my entire life for her, and now she was acting like I didn't exist.

The isolation plunged me deeper in to my depression; nights were unbearable. I remember falling asleep for an hour or two, only to wake up, staring into the darkness, unable to drift off again. No matter what I tried, I couldn't sleep. This went on for several months, three long months of relentless exhaustion. I started to wonder how long a person could survive on such little sleep. My mind ceased to function normally and I found myself in a permanent mental daze.

During the day, I worked as an electrician, but I have no idea how I managed to get through each shift. I moved through my days like a zombie, and it's a miracle that nothing terrible ever happened. I could have easily hurt myself or someone else. The smartest decision would have been to step away from the situation, but I couldn't bring myself to make that choice. My life was unraveling around me, and my mental resilience was stretched to its absolute limit. It felt like only a matter of time before something, or someone, snapped.

Desperate, I returned to the doctor. He prescribed sleeping pills, but they barely worked. For a few nights, I managed a couple of hours of sleep, but soon, the pills lost their effect. We cycled through different medications, but nothing help, in fact things only got worse. My life became an endless loop of sleepless nights and miserable days. I felt like a walking corpse, my mind clouded, my body depleted.

As I continued down this dark path, I began questioning the risks of the medication. The warning labels were frightening. One side effect stood out to me more than any other; "may cause death or suicidal thoughts and actions." The irony wasn't lost on me.

"If the pills don't kill me," I thought bitterly, "they'll make me want to kill myself." And they did.

I spiraled into an abyss of despair, trapped in a mental fog that obscured all rational thought. Dark, persistent thoughts began to take over. I couldn't explain why they haunted me so relentlessly, but they did.

The feeling of being trapped became unbearable. There was no way out of the nightmare I was living. I told Jan that the pills were making me want to hurt myself, but she just brushed it off, as if it was just what she wanted to hear. I told her I needed to come off of the medication, but she told me she would have me committed if I did. She even went to the extent of counting all of my pills on a daily basis to ensure I was taking the dreadful pills as prescribed.

Trapped in an unending limbo of numb despair, life felt utterly devoid of flavor, color, or meaning. It was as if nothing mattered, yet I was consumed by an overwhelming need to break free from this suffocating void. I felt trapped and helpless. Finally, one night, I decided I had reached my limit. Sleep, by any means necessary, became my goal. I marched to the bedroom with a singular purpose, rest, no matter the cost. I observed my bottle of sleeping pills and realized they were the answer, but a dark and terrible one. I stared at them for a long moment.

With my world in utter shambles, and my mind destroyed, it was time to act. The only thing I felt I could control was what I took inside me. I was determined to sleep that night. As I walked around the room I tried my best to come up with another answer other than the pill. They began to call to me, beckon for me to take them as my only means of escape. I resisted for a short time, but it wasn't long until my weakened mind surrendered to the call.

I picked up the bottle, knowing the danger that lay within, but at a point that I didn't care anymore. I downed a handful of pills and waited; nothing. I took another third of the remaining bottle. Still, I felt nothing. Frustrated, I took half the remaining bottle, convinced that this time it would work. But still, I lay there, wide awake. In a final act of desperation, I swallowed the rest of the pills.

Surely, there was no way I could stay awake now. Exhausted, I laid my head down, not caring about the consequences. Finally, the darkness closed in. I welcomed it, thinking it would bring me the peace of sleep. But what I found wasn't peace, it wasn't sleep, it was nothingness. Black, dark, and full of nothing but emptiness.

Some people talk about seeing a tunnel of light when they die, or being greeted by loved ones who have passed. For me, there was nothing. Just blackness. A void that swallowed me whole, as if I no longer existed. To this day, it's one of the most terrifying experiences I've ever had, knowing that I had disappeared into that darkness, and that there was nothing beyond it. That thought, the realization of nothingness, haunts me still. I had hoped to sleep for a night, but I had pushed things too far.

I was dead

Chapter 73

Despite everything I experienced, I still have to believe our lives don't simply end at death. I can't fully explain what happened to me during that time of darkness. I truly hope the reasons for my lack of memories of the experience are due to them simply being wiped away, or perhaps there's something else beyond my lack of comprehension. The only way I've come to grips with it is by realizing that no matter what happens after we die, we have no control over it. That helplessness has given me an unexpected motivation to live fully in the present. If there truly is nothing after this life, then every moment we have is that much more precious, a gift we can't afford to waste.

Maybe that's what I was supposed to learn. Perhaps this near-death experience was a way to remind me to stop taking life for granted, to take it more seriously. It's strange to think that something so traumatic could also be a gift.

Two days after I died, I saw a short flash of light. It was like I was in a momentary dream where I knew people were around me, but I didn't know who they were or where I was. What seemed like hours later, in this timeless void, I saw another flash of light. This time it lasted longer and I was able to retain more but it was still too short to make heads or tales of my situation. These flashes continued for about a day and got longer with each experience. Eventually, I woke up in the hospital, groggy and confused. I was surprised to find Jan sitting by my side, her expression unreadable.

"That was a close call," the doctor said when he noticed I was awake.

"What are you talking about?" I asked, my voice weak. "Where am I?"

"You're in the hospital," he replied, checking my vitals. "You overdosed on prescription medication. You're lucky to be alive."

The words hit me like a freight train, but it was the look on Jan's face that unsettled me the most. After the doctor left, I turned to her.

"What's going on?" I asked, trying to make sense of it all.

Her eyes met mine, cold and distant. "You died," she said flatly.

I stared at her in disbelief. "What?"

"You died," she repeated. "The doctor saved you."

There was something in her tone, something bitter, almost disappointed, as if she had wanted me to stay dead. The realization sent a chill down my spine. I had escaped death, but now I had to face my broken life again, and it felt worse than before.

Jan had several documents prepared for me to sign. My mind still wasn't completely clear so I still didn't fully understand what was happening. Jan and I had always keep separate bank accounts and had chose from the beginning to keep our money completely separate. It was in this moment that Jan decided it was time to change this policy and wanted complete control over my personal bank accounts.

Trusting that she had my best interests at heart, I signed them without much question. A day or two later, I discovered the money from my accounts was quickly being drained. When I realized my accounts were in jeopardy, I made several calls to determine what my options were. I froze the accounts immediately to protect what was left of my finances.

I hadn't heard from Jan in almost a week, but once she found out what I had done, she called and threatened me. Her way of speaking was so persuasive that I often felt powerless. Trapped in the hospital due to the circumstances that had landed me there, I was left with no way out. Jan abandoned me, and I couldn't be released without someone taking responsibility for me.

When my parents learned about my situation, they petitioned to have me released into their custody. But when Jan discovered this, she called my mom and shockingly Jan told her she wished I had stayed dead. My mom, the kindest person I've ever known, had never wished harm on anyone. But in that moment, her anger overwhelmed her. She was so furious that she wished Jan ill, something I'd never thought I'd witness from her. I didn't blame her.

I spent two weeks recovering in the hospital, time dragging on while I contemplated what I would do when I was finally discharged. When I was released, Jan was ready for me. But instead of taking me home, she handed me a plane ticket.

"You're flying back to Washington to be with your parents," she said.

I blinked, stunned. "What about my cars? My things?"

I had just bought a new car before I met Jan, my first and only new car. It was protected by the prenuptial agreement, and I didn't want to lose it.

"Don't worry, I'll send them up to you," she said dismissively.

"I'm not leaving without my stuff," I insisted.

Jan gave a small, almost smug smile. “Everything’s already been moved while you were in the hospital. The apartment is empty. All your things are gone.”

It felt like she had ripped my life away, right out from under me. Everything I owned, everything I cared about, was now in her control. I realized I had no choice but to take the plane ticket. Even if I tried to fight for my things, I wouldn’t find them. Jan wasn’t going to let me retrieve anything, and if I pushed, she’d likely call the police and have me arrested again.

So, I flew back to Washington, back to my parents’ home with nothing but a suitcase. A week later, Jan filed for divorce, and I hired movers to retrieve what remained of my property. But when my belongings arrived, many of them were broken, missing, or destroyed. Jan had taken everything she had wanted from my belongings.

Thousands of dollars’ worth of personal possessions, but more importantly, things with priceless sentimental value. Some these items included: my grandfather’s World War II sword, the two-dollar bill he gave me before he died, my daughter’s baby book, my son’s first lock of hair, yearbooks, family videos, my letterman’s jacket, my military uniforms, and my magic and hypnosis equipment. She took both of my cars, including my one and only brand-new car, my pride and joy. They were all gone.

I calculated the financial loss at nearly $100,000, but the emotional damage was far greater. Several of my damaged belongings were beyond repair, and I spent countless hours trying to salvage what I could. But it was clear, Jan hadn’t just wanted to hurt me, she wanted to erase me. She had taken everything she wanted and demolished what was left.

I never thought someone could be so cruel, so hateful. The things she did weren't just acts of malice, they were evil, pure and simple. I was left to pick up the pieces of my shattered life once again, but this time, it felt like there was almost nothing left to rebuild. I was going to have to start from scratch.

Chapter 74

Now that I was separated from Jan, I decided it was time to find out the truth about her. Something I should have done before we were married. It seemed I couldn't get it from her, so I did my own research into the facts. When we first got married, she told me I was her second husband. At the time, I had no reason to doubt her. But as the months passed, her story began to unravel. Eventually, she confessed I wasn't her second husband at all. She admitted I was her third, but that wasn't true either.

Even then, something didn't sit right with me, and now I began to dig deeper. What I discovered was far worse than I could have imagined. According to county records, I was Jan's sixth husband. I was floored. How could someone hide that many marriages, let alone go through them in such rapid succession?

As I pieced together the fragments of her past, I realized a troubling pattern. Most of Jan's marriages lasted only a few months. They were brief, whirlwind romances that ended abruptly, often with her filing restraining orders against her husbands. And each time, it seemed, she walked away with most of their possessions.

It became clear this was part of a cycle, one she repeated over and over. It wasn't just about the marriages, though. Jan had a knack for manipulation and coercion that went far beyond her husbands. I was horrified to discover she had something on her boss as well, forcing him to pay her $8,000. She was shady about the details, and while I couldn't get the full story, whatever she held over him must have been significant.

I suspected it was some kind of blackmail, perhaps she'd found out something about him that he couldn't afford to let become public. Given what I had discovered about Jan, it could have been just about anything. Jan's ability to twist situations to her advantage left me shaken, and I realized how little I truly knew about the person I had married.

* * *

My life was in ruins once again, but fortunately, my family was there to lift me out of the pit of despair. I don't know what I would have done without their unwavering support. On more than one occasion, I'd fallen hard, and each time, my parents were there to help me back on my feet. I realize now just how fortunate I am to have that kind of safety net, a luxury not everyone is lucky enough to have. I didn't always appreciate my parents when I was younger, but after everything I've been through, I cherish them more every day.

The first step in getting my life back on track was to throw out all of the medications that had spiraled me into even darker places. They had only made a bad situation worse, and I was determined never to go down that path again. Next, I focused on rebuilding my life, starting with work. I went back to work as an electrician, threw myself into saving up money, and found solace in the routine.

Family had always been my anchor, a strong foundation that I could rely on. We love each other deeply and would go to great lengths to support one another. My sister Kristen had been married for twelve years by this point, with two wonderful kids. She and I shared a special bond, one that felt stronger than any other connection I had. I loved her dearly, in the purest brotherly way, and she was a constant source of support.

My brother, Sean, was also married and had five children of his own. A devoutly moral man, he has often been the voice of reason in my life. Ted had moved back in with our parents after losing his condo in the financial crisis. Our family was large, close-knit, and always together. My nieces and nephews were constantly at my parents' house, filling the space with laughter and the chaos only kids can bring. We love spending time with them, teaching them things, and playing silly games. Family gatherings during Thanksgiving and Christmas are never missed, and those moments are the highlight of our lives.

Through every storm I've weathered, my family has been my anchor. In those moments of joy spent with them, I realized that even when life falls apart, they would always be there to help me rebuild. Our bond is unbreakable, and in the face of all I've lost, I've gained something invaluable; love.

Starting over wasn't new to me. It had, however, become a pattern I wished I could break. I guess if you don't learn the lesson, life finds a way to repeat it. So now, with a miracle, and the unwavering support of my parents and family, I have another shot at living fully. My goal is simple; to make the most of this second chance.

Sometimes, you don't realize what you have until it's slipping away. I thought I had nothing left to lose, but now I see I was wrong. As long as there's breath in our lungs, there's hope, and it's never too late to build something meaningful. Hindsight makes it easy to see where I could have done better; in the moment, it's a different story. My goal now is to do better, and hopefully, with time, I will.

To Be Continued

About the Author

Joe Black is an author, magician, and hypnotist based in Washington State, who has performed as a professional entertainer since 1996. A few years after beginning his career, Joe founded his own entertainment company and now serves as the CEO of Black Magic Entertainment. Before venturing into the entertainment industry, he honorably served for six years in the United States Marine Corps.

In addition to his work as an entertainer, Joe is a prolific writer and has authored several books, including;

- The Spirit Among Us
- The Spirit of Revenge
- The Last Vampire
- The Wrath of Lucious
- Paradox
- Pat the Panther

For more about his work, visit BlackMagicEntertainment.com.

Made in the USA
Middletown, DE
26 November 2024